MW00618709

TO
RUSSIA
WITH LOVE

SCRIPTURE'S SECRET INVASION
OF THE COMMUNIST SOVIET UNION

The true story of HANS KRISTIAN as told to
DAVE HUNT

The Berean Call

BEND • OREGON

THE BEREAN CALL is grateful to Dave Hunt and Hans Kristian for the privilege of preserving this remarkable testimony of God's faithfulness to those who willingly forsake all and take up the cross daily to fulfill our Lord's great commission. It is our prayer that this valuable historical record will inspire a new generation of Spirit-filled missionaries to "go... and teach all nations" the good news of the Gospel of Christ Jesus.

ABOUT THE PUBLISHER:

The Berean Call (TBC) is a nonprofit, tax-exempt corporation which exists to:

ALERT believers in Christ to unbiblical teachings and practices impacting the church

EXHORT believers to give greater heed to biblical discernment and truth regarding teachings and practices being currently promoted in the church

SUPPLY believers with teaching, information, and materials which will encourage the love of God's truth, and assist in the development of biblical discernment

MOBILIZE believers in Christ to action in obedience to the scriptural command to "earnestly contend for the faith" (Jude 3)

IMPACT the church of Jesus Christ with the necessity for trusting the Scriptures as the only rule for faith, practice, and a life pleasing to God

A free monthly newsletter, THE BEREAN CALL, *may be received by sending a request to the address below, or by calling 1-800-937-6638. To register for free e-mail updates, to access our digital archives, and to order a variety of additional resource materials online, visit us at: www. thebereancall.org*

Contents

Foreword

Most people are too strong to be used by a strong God.
Or too smart.
But you don't have to be smart when you are right.
Nor strong.

Is that why Hans Kristian is what he is and does what he is doing? The first time I met him (as it happened, in Sweden, at a Slavic Mission Conference on "the work for the Communist countries"), I did not think much of him, leaning heavily as he was on his walking stick, severely handicapped because of a recent stroke, with his broken English, and, well—just that.

But how does God work? C.T. Studd, founder of the Worldwide Evangelization Crusade, said:

Despise not men nor things
　however weak or small.
God loves to choose,
　and mightily use
What men count nothing at all.

How does God work? Through very ordinary men and women who have chosen to love Jesus above all else and to obey God rather than men. (And how practically necessary that is once you have caught the vision of the Iron Curtain lands and at the same time you have a lovely family.) Those who still debate the morality of doing so-called illegal things will have to do a lot of explaining when it comes to Acts 5:29. It is not just a verse, it is a principle. The most illegal action which Jesus ever committed was done on Easter morning when He broke the official government seal and came out of the grave. Are there any believers who object to that grand act?

To love Jesus above all else, and to obey God rather than men—these are the two qualifications for the enormous task. God's power *is* made perfect in weakness and we do grow strong in the battle. That is why we do not have to be strong at the start—not as individual believers in Jesus Christ, nor as a mission.

We should once and for all settle the thought that any of us could possibly outsmart those trained customs officers. I for one would not try to do it. So you don't have to be smart. Let's get back to the fundamentals. God is so great! The world is so big! The need is so overwhelming! Revolution is so terribly threatening! Persecution of the church is so deplorable! Governments and many politicians are so corrupt! And all that is because people do not know and love Jesus!

On the other side stand those who are willing to put their lives on the line because they do know and love Jesus—not because they are strong or smart. It will indeed be by the foolishness of the preaching of the gospel that all devil-inspired, man-made barriers will one day fall, to give way to the kingdom of God. You are right, Hans Kristian.

Gladly your fellow smuggler,
Brother Andrew

Prologue

I gathered much of the information for writing this book at a Bible smugglers conference in Sweden. Hans Kristian had stayed with our family in California the year before, and during that visit I had learned to love and respect him as a man of God who was firm in his commitment to Christ and courageous in fulfilling that commitment no matter what the cost might be. Knowing of our previous travels behind the Iron Curtain and our keen interest in his work, Hans had invited us to attend this unusual gathering sponsored by several Dutch, German, and Scandinavian missions working together in Eastern Europe.

That week in Sweden was like being in another world. Here were the men and women whom God was using in a secret invasion of Communist countries that most Christians were not even aware was in progress. I met heroes and heroines of the faith whose names were unknown outside of this clandestine fellowship. The stories they told—modestly and factually, giving God the glory—rivaled the exploits of Old Testament prophets or the early Christians in the Book of Acts.

Somehow the story had to be told to the church in the West. That conviction became my passion. The details were secret and some names would have to be changed. But Christians throughout the Western world had to know that this invasion was in progress.

Only then could they join forces, through prayer and financial help, with those who were taking the risks on the front lines in a battle that was crucial to the survival of the church in half of the world. Through whose eyes would the story be told? Who would trust me to tell it, since I was really an outsider?

Only two people at the conference knew me: Hans Kristian, of course, and Brother Andrew, whom I had first met ten years before in Amsterdam. His book, *God's Smuggler*, had powerfully impacted the church. But there was so much more to say. After earnest prayer, Hans agreed to let me tell his story to the church and to the world.

I interviewed the man who went with Hans on his very first trip into Eastern Europe and talked with many who knew Hans and had worked with him. I spoke with couriers who were crossing Communist borders on a regular basis and interviewed the heads of several mission groups. With tape recorder running I spent day after day with Hans—first in Sweden, then in Copenhagen, and later on when he visited us in France where we were living at the time.

I warn you that the following pages will change your thinking and perhaps your life. Much will seem unbelievable—but it is all true. If you are an atheist or skeptic, your belief that God does not exist will be shaken and quite possibly shattered. If you are not a Christian you will perhaps become one, as so many others have through reading this true story. And if you are a Christian, your faith will be strengthened and your life challenged. Whoever you are, you cannot help but be moved, both in sorrow and in joy, as you read on.

This is not the story of Dave Hunt—I am only the narrator. It is Hans Kristian's story, and I have told it in the first person so that you can experience it just the way he lived it.

—Dave Hunt
Los Angeles, California

SECRET INVASION

1

What Law Forbids This?

Looking straight ahead through the windshield and past the low barrier blocking the road in front of us, I could see the long, narrow bridge over the River Bug. Poland lay on the other side. Just beyond the barrier, in the no-man's-land between us and the bridge, suitcases were being shoved back into a Volvo after a brief examination by Russian customs. Three cars had been lined up there when we had arrived thirty minutes before, and I couldn't understand why the guard had kept us waiting—unless they intended to clear the customs complex of other tourists before admitting us. That seemed unusual, but I attached no special significance to the idea. Neither speculation nor impatience availed when one faced the vagaries of Communist border crossings.

One last exposure remained in my camera. I had been struggling with the temptation to take a picture of the guard when he wasn't looking—a classic shot with the border station and bridge in the background—but prudence had finally won. That would be asking for trouble.

As the Volvo began moving slowly toward the bridge, the telephone beside the barrier jangled sharply. The guard lifted the receiver, listened for a moment, and raised the steel gate. I eased the car carefully through the steep dip in the road, then picked up as much speed as I dared for the two hundred yards to the customs building. It was getting late and we had a long drive ahead of us to reach the hotel in Poland where we had planned to spend the night. I hoped the border check would be faster than usual this time.

Although I was an old hand at traveling in Eastern Europe, this had been my first trip into Russia. A kaleidoscope of varying impressions had crowded into my memory, leaving me with a feeling of mental indigestion that I knew from experience would sort itself out in retrospect. There were the many churches that I had photographed, still being closed down by the Soviet government, some even turned into museums for the promotion of atheism; the tears in so many eyes and the expressions of joy on the believers' faces as we had given them Bibles; the extreme difficulty in making any contact with the ordinary citizen; the indescribable feeling of vastness that turned into frustration under the rigid rules proclaiming most of Russia off-limits to tourists; the control zones everywhere with signs telling us to slow to forty kilometers per hour so that our license number could be ticked off the schedule, thus showing that we were on route and within the time allowed from the previous checkpoint; the oppressive feeling of always being under the ever-watchful eye of the state.

It had been a good trip and I was glad that we had come—but I was also glad we were leaving. I always had that feeling in an Eastern European country, but I felt it especially strongly now. More enigmatic and unpredictable, Russia had its own peculiar mystique. This was where the movement that now controlled half of the world had first begun. It gave me a feeling of awe just to think of that.

"Feels good to be leaving, doesn't it?" I said to Bent

Jacobson, the treasurer of our mission and my traveling companion on this, his first trip into Eastern Europe.

He nodded without comment. I knew what he was thinking: We weren't out yet. But that should be no problem. It seldom was.

Two armed guards motioned me to stop the car in front of a long, low, frame structure that looked like a converted barracks. It seemed out of place next to the solid, stone building standing square and tall just beyond and a few yards nearer Poland. Two pairs of eyes watched impassively as Bent and I climbed out and stretched our cramped muscles.

"*Guten Tag,*" I said to the guard on my side of the car.

If he understood German he gave no indication. There was no relaxation of the stern expression on his face. Not the flicker of an eyelid.

The same tall, thin, boyish Intourist interpreter who had tried so hard to be friendly when we had entered Russia at this same point hurried out of the red stone headquarters and over to our car. Then it had been, "Hello! I'm your friend from Intourist. May I help you?" Now the warm smile he had greeted us with was missing.

"You are ordered to empty your car and bring everything inside," he said brusquely in English, motioning toward the frame building and hurrying into it ahead of us.

"That's not too unusual," I muttered to Bent in Danish as we pulled our suitcases, cameras, and sleeping bags from the back seat and trunk.

Entering the reception room with our arms full, we both immediately noticed that there seemed to be more than the usual number of officials inside. A tall, red-faced man in a green police uniform, gesturing angrily, was talking in a loud, explosive voice to five uniformed customs officers standing in a tight group around him. Although I couldn't understand Russian, the cold stares turned upon us gave me an uneasy feeling that we were somehow the subject of their conversation.

We dumped our belongings onto a long table, typical of customs offices, and for lack of further instructions, stood there waiting.

Glancing outside, I saw that the two guards were now searching our car thoroughly. That gave me little concern. On the way into Russia, four guards had searched the car for three hours, using screwdrivers to take the door panels off and literally pulling the car apart with their tools, but they had not found the Bibles we had been carrying. We had asked God to hide them from their eyes. Now there was no longer anything to hide, at least not in the car. I tried to tell myself that there was also nothing to fear— but that feeling of uneasiness was growing stronger.

"May we change our money?" I asked in English, addressing no one in particular. The Intourist guide conferred briefly with the angry man in the green uniform, who seemed to be a visiting high officer there for a special occasion.

"Be sure your suitcases are unlocked first," we were told.

"They're open," I replied.

Going outside, Bent and I walked the few yards from the frame annex to the solid, stone headquarters and entered. A matronly woman seated in a small office behind a glass marked CHANGE seemed to be the only one in the building.

"Dollars, please," I said in German, sliding our rubles toward her under the glass. I remembered that she couldn't speak English.

"We have no dollars."

"But I gave you dollars for these rubles when we entered right here!"

She shrugged. "We're out of dollars right now. I'll give you Polish money and maybe you can get dollars over the border."

I gave her a skeptical smile of reproof. This game had been played with me so many times. These countries were always short of dollars, because no one would accept their currencies in payment of international trade. We would have to settle for another western currency.

"What else do you have?"

"How about English pounds—or Swedish kroner?"

"We would prefer Danish kroner. But if you don't have it, we'll take Swedish."

She calculated the exchange rate, counted out the kroner, and gave us a receipt. We were just turning to leave when the front door opened and the red-faced officer, who seemed to be perpetually angry, came storming in, followed by the young Intourist interpreter.

"You come with us," said the angry officer through the interpreter, pointing to me. "You wait outside," he said to Bent.

Following them through a doorway, I was led down a narrow hall to an office in the rear. A short, muscular, dark-skinned man, who seemed partially oriental like so many of the Russians from the East, looked up from behind his desk as though he had been waiting for us. Then to my horror, I saw three Bibles laid out in front of him, two of them in clear plastic bags. They looked frighteningly like the ones we had been giving out—but how could they be here? Had we been betrayed?

Taking a deep breath and letting it out slowly, I tried to exercise mental control over my pounding heart and the warm flush I could feel in my face.

A few words were spoken in Russian by the tall officer, then he turned on his heels and left me with the short, dark man and the interpreter.

The uniformed officer behind the desk fixed me with an indignant stare and spoke to me in Russian, gesturing toward the Bibles. The interpreter, now sitting beside him, translated.

"Are these your Bibles?"

"No, they are not."

"Are you a Christian?"

"Yes."

"Is it allowed for Christians to lie?"

"No, it is not. A Christian must always speak the truth."

"You are a Christian, you brought these Bibles into Russia, and you say they are not yours?" His voice was swelling with anger.

"No, they are not mine."

"What do you mean!" he shouted, slamming his hand on the desk.

"We brought those Bibles as gifts to the Russian people," I replied slowly, trying to keep calm. The indignant expression on his face was unnerving. "When you give something away, it isn't yours anymore, is it?"

"Then you admit you brought these Bibles!"

I nodded and swallowed hard. "Yes, that's true. But what's wrong with bringing Bibles as gifts?"

"It is forbidden by law!" He shook his fist at me to emphasize that last word.

"But I thought you had religious freedom in your country. That's what you advertise."

"Of course we do. You Christians in the West tell lies about us, but everyone in the Soviet Union is allowed to practice his own religion. This is guaranteed by our constitution."

"That is exactly what I thought," I replied, trying to smile and giving up the attempt. "Then it must be allowed for Christians to have their handbook, the Bible."

"That's true, but it is forbidden to bring Bibles into the country."

"What law forbids this?" I asked sincerely. "Can you give me the number of it?"

He made no reply.

"If this is forbidden," I insisted, "then you should plainly tell us before we come!"

"You were told in the regulations you got with your application for the visa." His face had clouded with anger again. "If you read them, which you are required to do, then you know it is forbidden to bring in literature harmful to our system!"

As he spoke, I was praying silently for wisdom to give the right answer.

"Don't you print Bibles in your country?" I asked innocently. I knew that they printed a few, mainly for propaganda purposes.

He glared at me in angry silence.

"I have read statistics," I persisted, "published by the Central Committee stating that the Soviet government prints Bibles. I can't believe that you would print something that is harmful to your own system!"

"I have no time to waste arguing over technicalities!" he exploded in anger, half rising from his chair. Then he sank back and said in a calmer voice, "Let's come to the point. If you were doing an honest work, then why did you hide the Bibles so we couldn't find them when you passed the border coming in?"

"Why did I hide them?" I repeated, stalling for time while I sent up a quick prayer for wisdom, not knowing how to answer such a question. Strange that I had never anticipated it. The verse in Matthew flashed through my mind where Christ said: When you are arrested for my sake, don't worry about how to answer your accusers. I will tell you what to say in that very same moment.

"I also brought money into your country," I replied slowly. "That is not against the law, is it—to bring money with me?"

He shook his head. Folding his arms, he leaned back and waited.

Pulling my coat open, I reached into the inside pocket and took out my wallet.

"I also hide my money—here in my wallet, inside my coat," I continued. "Even though it is not against the law to carry money. Because I know that if I don't hide it, there are thieves and robbers who will try to take it away from me!"

His face had been growing darker with rage as I spoke. "*You* are the thief!" he screamed, leaning across the desk. "You came as a spy! But we caught you!"

Simmering down, his eyes narrowed. He pointed to the Bibles on the desk. "What about the others? Who did you give them to?"

"Oh, I can't remember Russian names. . . ."

"In what towns?"

"Well, we gave some away in Smolensk, in Minsk—several towns. Wherever we went."

"The Russian people don't want this religious propaganda. Our parents were backward peasants under the Czars, but the revolution has changed all that. Our scientists have disproved those myths." There was a look of disgust on his face.

I shrugged. "The ones we gave Bibles to received them with great joy."

"That's because they're Christians," he replied indignantly. Then his eyes narrowed again. "How did you find the Christians?"

"Oh, it's universal in every language to say hallelujah. When we say hallelujah, the Christians are glad and the Communists are angry, so we can tell easily which ones are Christians."

An unwilling smile seemed to be tugging at the corners of his mouth, and then the expression on his face became very solemn once more. "You know that you have broken our laws. . . ."

"I have broken no laws," I interrupted. "You admit there is no law that forbids bringing Bibles!"

"You have come as a spy, a thief, and a robber!" he exclaimed, ignoring my protest. "You have brought in propaganda harmful to our system. This is a very serious crime. And you refuse to tell us the names of the people who received these poisonous myths!"

He stood up and walked out of the room abruptly, leaving me alone with the interpreter. I spent the time trying to figure out how they could have gotten those Bibles there ahead of us. Realizing that we were nearing the border, and still having eight Bibles, we had put them into plastic bags and Bent had dropped them beside paths leading from the road to villages where we were not allowed to go. We had been so careful not to be observed and our only stop after that had been a few minutes to purchase gas. Then how could these Bibles have been discovered and carried to the border before we got there?

Pondering that question without finding an answer left me with a new feeling of admiration for the efficiency of the Russian police.

My questioner returned, accompanied by the high officer with the perpetually red face. The latter stood in the doorway, while the short, dark man came around behind his desk and faced me with an icy stare. There was a faint smile on his lips.

"You're under arrest!" he said dramatically. "You will wait outside while we talk to your friend."

A spasm of fear shot through me, and then I recovered my composure. He had to be bluffing. Under arrest? I had broken no law. They had found three Bibles beside the road, nothing more. He was trying to frighten me—and I determined not to give him the satisfaction of seeing fear in my eyes.

Bent was being brought in as I walked out. It was impossible to say anything to him. I wondered what his reaction would be when he saw those Bibles on the desk.

Pacing back and forth outside, I suddenly remembered our one remaining Russian New Testament, still in my coat pocket. Quickly I hid it under my shirt against my back, just above the belt.

When they had finished with Bent, we were led back into the other building. Our belongings had been carefully arranged into several piles. The interpreter told us we could put toilet articles and a change of underwear back into the suitcases, but everything else would have to remain for further examination.

"What do you mean?" I demanded.

"You aren't leaving Russia yet!"

The tall officer in charge, whom I had mentally nicknamed the Great Angry One, motioned for me to lift my arms. He began searching me, going through my pockets and emptying anything except money onto the table, then patting his hands along my shirt under my coat. One hand went around my waist from each side. I stiffened involuntarily. The hands came back without quite reaching the New Testament. The same process was completed on Bent.

My briefcase had been emptied of all my papers, which were sorted out neatly on the table into small stacks. I tried to remember what was in them, but it was hopeless even to think about it. I saw my Danish concordance and some other books in Danish and German, stacked together on the table. Then I noticed that my Bible was with them.

"That's my own Bible—a Danish one!" I protested, pointing to it. "You can't keep that! I want to have my Bible!"

"That's religious propaganda—it's forbidden," came the reply in an impassive voice.

"But we're Danish citizens, and we *must* have our Bibles," Bent and I both insisted.

The Great Angry One appeared to be on the verge of an explosion. *"Nyet!"* he yelled with finality, and turned away.

"Listen!" I pleaded. "The Bible means more to me than the words of Lenin mean to you. Please let me have it!"

He turned quickly around in surprise, and a look of respect came slowly into his face.

"Okay," he said abruptly, "give them their Danish Bibles."

An officer riffled through my Bible but found nothing. He handed it to me. Picking up Bent's, he held it upside down, and shook it hard. A waterfall of papers cascaded down onto the table. A guard pounced upon them with a grunt of satisfaction and gathered them together into a neat pile. After riffling through Bent's Bible several more times to be sure it was empty, the officer handed it to him.

Seeing those papers falling onto the table had started my heart pounding heavily, especially when I caught sight of the letterhead of the mission I had founded. I thought we had been careful to have nothing "incriminating" in our possession. As the papers were being gathered together, I noticed several newsletters about radio broadcasts into Russia that mentioned other Scandinavian missions working in Eastern Europe. Suddenly, for the first time during our detention, I was afraid.

The interpreter's voice interrupted my thoughts. The Great Angry One was addressing us. "You're under arrest! Change your money back to rubles! Then the Intourist guide will show you the hotel where you must remain. Don't be foolish and try to leave. There's nowhere to go. Tomorrow a special team will arrive to question you. Wait for them in your room."

Sitting in the backseat, the Intourist guide directed me through the cobblestone streets of Brest. My anxiety was almost forgotten in the excitement I felt at being in a forbidden city. My eyes darted everywhere, searching in vain for the reason why this town—like the entire Soviet Union except for a few large cities—is strictly off-limits to foreign tourists. Travel by car between approved cities is restricted to the main highway, and it is forbidden to stop beside the road along the way, even momentarily.

I was told to park in front of an old hotel that apparently had been quite luxurious in its day, and was undoubtedly still the finest in this drab town. Constructed of gray stones, now covered by the smoke of years, it stood on a square and seemed to be quite popular with Russian travelers. My emotions were fluctuating between anger and fear. I felt helpless. After parking the car, I turned to the Intourist guide sitting behind me.

"We came to your country as tourists," I said sternly. "And we have been treated like criminals and placed under arrest, although we have broken no laws. I'm going to publish this to the world so that everyone will know how you treat tourists!"

He shrugged and led us inside. After helping us to register, he reminded us that we must be in our room when the officials arrived to question us the next morning. Apparently they were coming from another city.

The room was small, with twin beds crowded into it, and a toilet and washbasin in one corner. Putting our suitcases down on the floor, Bent and I sat on the beds facing one another. For the first time I realized how exhausted I was—and hungry. The man behind the desk could speak German and told us we might find something to eat at the railway station if we hurried. During the short walk to and from the station, we discussed the questions that each of us had been asked and the answers we had given, and speculated about what would take place in the morning. We both agreed that we would not lie but also that we would not betray the identity of anyone to whom we had given a Bible.

Back in the hotel with some food in our stomachs, we felt a little more cheerful. Not knowing whether the room might be bugged, we avoided discussing our case, but read the Bible aloud, prayed, and sang until after midnight. The only thing we could do now was to wait and see what would happen.

After we had turned out the lights, I lay awake for a long time, troubled by fruitless attempts to understand the real implications of our arrest. It was ridiculous even to imagine that we might be put in prison for what we had done. But this was Russia, and that meant anything could happen. We were at their mercy. I knew it was common to be imprisoned without a trial. No one would even know where we were, perhaps for months. If we hadn't returned in a reasonable time, our wives would frantically inquire. But we had visited several countries, and it could be very difficult to discover where we were until the Soviets were ready to publicize our case. Such a thing would be impossible in Denmark, but this was Russia. Slowly but surely the awesome reality of what that could mean was beginning to grip me.

I thought of the car. Suppose it were confiscated? And my photos! They were so special! I *had* to get them out of Russia. There was such a controversy in the West about the existence of an underground church. Now I had the evidence. In the town of Smolensk, where, typically, the authorities had closed 90 percent of the churches, and were still closing more, I had taken pictures of factories, retail stores, government offices, warehouses, and museums that had once been churches. Those pictures would dispel all doubts! Should the congregations of closed churches give up their faith? It was forbidden to worship God, sing hymns, or discuss the Bible, except in licensed churches. Where those were closed, the Christians were forced to go underground.

"Oh, God," I prayed, "please don't let them confiscate those films! And that car, Lord, it cost so much...."

Then I realized the obvious fact that if they put Bent and me in prison, what happened to the car and the films was a foregone conclusion.

I wasn't sure that I could ask the Lord to set me free. I knew the Scripture well: Pray for them in bonds as bound with them. I had often wondered how I could do that, since I had never experienced prison myself. Should I shrink now from this, if it was God's will? The Christians in Russia were willing to go to prison for Christ. Should I be willing to do less?

A great struggle was going on within. My heart had become a battlefield between opposing desires. Questions without answers battered my confused and weary mind. How had I gotten involved in such a ministry? Was it really God's will, or something that I had decided?

I began mentally to retrace the steps that had brought me to that very hotel room in which I now lay, under arrest, at the Russian-Polish border. It had all started with a book that led me to a desk full of letters, each containing the same desperate appeal—an appeal for help that had changed the course of my life.

2

Give Us Bibles

"So few people are willing to admit that Europe is a mission field!" exclaimed an elderly Belgian pastor to me one day early in 1965. "Americans, British, Australians, Scandinavians have come here year after year for language study on their way to a mission assignment in Africa. While teaching French, I have tried to persuade them that France and Belgium need missionaries more than the countries they are going to, and I have begged them to use their French in Europe."

His face was stamped with an expression not so much of annoyance as of mystification—the shocked incredulity of a man trying to analyze a defeat that should have been such an easy victory.

"Not one missionary candidate have I ever convinced—*not one!* They couldn't believe me. They were so oriented by all their previous training to think of a mission field in terms of nonwhites that they couldn't accept what I said no matter how much proof I offered. After all, Europe is so 'civilized.' "

I was wrestling at the time with this very issue.

Europe a mission field? Nonsense. European missionaries were evangelizing North and South America before
the United States even existed as a nation. Hadn't Europeans been the first to bring the gospel to Africa, India,
and China? The Reformation had been conceived and
brought to fruition by Europeans. The blood of the
martyrs had stained European soil—and weren't the ripen-
ing fruits of that holy struggle still with us, evidenced by
the church spires piercing the sky above every village,
no matter how small, throughout Europe?

Born and raised in Denmark, I was proud to be a
European, proud to live at the very hub and cradle of the
civilized world—home of famous philosophers, scientists,
inventors, explorers, and Christian leaders such as Calvin,
Luther, Wesley, Livingstone, Zwingli, Darby, Huss, and
Zinzendorf. The list was endless and could not be matched
in any other area of the world.

Of course we had our share of Voltaires, Darwins,
Marxes, and Bultmanns, but that would always be the
case everywhere. True enough, Europe had spawned two
world wars in a generation, and her skies had been
overcast with the smoke of six million Jews sacrificed to
the Aryan legend—but that did not detract from the fact
that Europe was a Christian continent, or at least as near
to one as possible in an imperfect world.

Such had been my thinking—if one could call it thinking
to accept something so obvious—when I picked up the
book by Dr. R.P. Evans, *Let Europe Hear*, toward the
end of 1964. At first I read in unbelief, even anger. Evans
was citing statistics, but how could they be accurate? He
said that France was 3 percent Protestant and 17 percent
Catholic, with only a small percentage of these actually
attending church regularly. He claimed that 80 percent
of the people in France professed no religious belief
(though spiritism was rampant, with more people licensed
to diagnose and treat disease by spiritual magnetism
than there were medical doctors). Most African nations,

he claimed, could boast of a higher percentage of practicing Christians than France, and Brazil had nearly thirty times as many Protestants as Spain, the country that had colonized it. The startling statistics went on and on.

The message of that book haunted me. If what Dr. Evans said was true, then Europe was in fact one of the largest and neediest mission fields in the world. Had I indeed been blind, deceived by the false vision of a Christian continent that had merely assumed the mask of an educated and civilized paganism? Such an important question had to be answered. Dr. Evans had stated his case—but I must see for myself.

So it was that in this uncertain frame of mind, shaken and challenged, driven by the necessity of knowing the truth about Europe's spiritual condition, I asked for, and received in early 1965, one month's leave of absence from the church I pastored in Jutland, Western Denmark. Traveling south into the heartland of Europe, I visited churches, interviewed Christian leaders, and pursued my research in libraries. The Belgian pastor mentioned above, president of a Bible school, was one of the first men I interviewed.

Researching and investigating on my own to verify Dr. Evan's thesis, I soon discovered that he had not overstated his case. For instance, in the region of Bavaria, in southern Germany, there are twelve million people. Scandinavia alone has sent one hundred fifty missionaries to Tanzania, a country with the same population, while sending none to Bavaria. And why? Because no one could force himself to think of Germany as a pagan country in need of missionaries. Its fifty-five million inhabitants at this time were roughly half Catholics and half Lutherans. Yet only 5 percent of the Protestants could be found in church on Sunday, and even those attending church, both Catholics and Protestants, did so more out of tradition than because of a living relationship with Christ. While they could recite the creed, went to confession, and took communion, any impartial observer following them outside the church would be forced to conclude that their religion left their lives, for the most part, indistinguishable from those of friends and neighbors who were atheists.

Such was the impotence of the Christianity that I discovered in Germany and throughout Western Europe.

Strangely enough, the possibility that conditions in Eastern Europe might be as bad—or even worse—had never occurred to me. Any thought I might have given to that part of the world was little more than a hazy admission of its existence on the other side of something called an Iron Curtain. That infamous barrier, whatever it was, apparently excluded any outside interference, conveniently relieving me of the responsibility of concerning myself with spiritual conditions beyond it. The other side of the Iron Curtain seemed as remote to me as the other side of the moon.

While pursuing my research in Paris, however, someone told me I must meet a certain pastor who had escaped from this unreal world behind the Curtain and who was living not far from the Eiffel Tower. Out of curiosity, I traveled across Paris to interview Jeremie Hodoroaba. Unfortunately he was away at the time, but his wife received me kindly and answered my questions. I was deeply moved by the things she told me, but of course completely unsuspecting that the information I received in that unpretentious apartment in Paris would change the entire course of my life. Much less could I have imagined that because of it, one day I would be under arrest in Russia!

Mrs. Hodoroaba was the first person who really aroused me to seriously consider the plight of Christians in Eastern Europe and especially the need they have for Bibles. She told me of her husband's weekly broadcasts of the gospel of Christ to their native Romania and explained that although it was forbidden to listen to transmissions from the West, nevertheless, thousands did. In spite of the government's determination to stamp out all religious belief, disillusionment with the failure of communism to create the promised paradise was causing even the younger generation to turn elsewhere in their pursuit of a solution to life's dilemmas. Many were turning to Christ.

While showing me through the studio where her husband recorded his messages, Mrs. Hodoroaba took me into his office to see the correspondence being received from Romania. She opened a file drawer and pulled out hundreds of letters. Spreading them out in front of me, she said, "These are only a few samples of the responses my husband receives from his broadcasts. And they all have one thing in common. Can you guess what it is?"

"I wouldn't have the slightest idea," I confessed, shaking my head.

"They all want Bibles!" Her eyes flashed. "There is one plea, one cry in every one of these letters: 'Please send us Bibles!' "

"Is there any way to do it?" I asked, feeling sudden concern for a need that I had not heard of before.

She nodded. "If sent by registered mail, most of them get through. But we don't have the funds...." She shrugged her shoulders helplessly and gestured toward the letters spread out on the desk. "And even if we did, it would take a full-time staff just to keep up with the requests. We do what we can, but it's nothing. If only some mission would take this on as a special project." She looked at me helplessly, appealingly.

"Maybe I could start a mission," I said suddenly, and then laughed at the thought, hoping she would understand that it was just a wild idea, the generous impulse of the moment. Why had I said it? And having said it, why should I feel so uncomfortable, as though I were shirking an obligation?

Staring at those letters written in a language I couldn't read, I heard myself say, "Perhaps I could write some articles for religious magazines. It might be a way at least to raise money."

Out of that hesitant statement, the new mission was destined to be born. By the time I reached home this half-formed idea had become a passion.

Staying up late night after night, laboring to express what I had seen and now felt so deeply, I tried to describe on paper what I had learned of Europe's spiritual bankruptcy, and of the desperate need for Bibles in Romania. Several Christian magazines in Denmark published my articles. I received angry letters from some of the readers, who insisted that anywhere in the world except Europe was a mission field. But the general response was an overwhelming willingness to face the facts and to do something about it.

People began to send me money to be used to support missionaries in Europe, and to mail Bibles into Romania. Believing that God was leading, I founded a mission under the auspices of my church board to account for these funds and to organize and implement missionary work for spreading the gospel in Europe. The first worker we began to support was in France. Others were gradually added.

However, it was the urgent need to supply Romanian Christians with Bibles that seemed to hold the strongest appeal with the majority of people who began to support our new work. Most of the money the new mission received was for this purpose. During the first two months more than $4,000 came in, designated for Romanian Bibles. An insignificant sum by most standards, but to me it was a larger response than I had imagined from my own small country of Denmark. The mission had no salaried workers, so that everything we received could be used entirely for the purpose intended.

Using addresses supplied by Pastor Hodoroaba, we started to send Bibles by registered mail into Romania to those who had requested them. The mission purchased the Bibles and paid the postage, but the actual mailing was done by volunteers who for obvious reasons used their own return addresses on the packages.

Letters from Romania, mostly unsigned, began arriving at the volunteers' homes, thanking them for the Bibles. Those who did sign their names expressed their appreciation without identifying what they had received: "Thank you for the beautiful present! It is the most wonderful gift anyone ever sent us!"

At the beginning, about one Bible out of every four was returned by the Romanian postal service. Wrapped in a new package and mailed again to the same address, usually three-fourths of these would reach their destination. We did this successfully for several months—then suddenly nearly all of the Bibles began to come back. The Romanian government had discovered that Bibles were being mailed from Denmark and would not let them through.

Discussing this problem together, we decided to see if mailing the Bibles from another country would suffice to get them by the Romanian authorities. A friend in Israel offered to help. I began to send Bibles and lists of names and addresses for him to spread among volunteers in his country. While the few Bibles we continued to mail from Denmark as an experiment were all returned, the ones being sent from Israel nearly all got through—for several months. Then they began coming back, also. Next we recruited volunteers in Sweden to mail the Bibles to Romania. Again they reached their destinations for several months before they, too, suddenly began coming back.

For almost two years we played our desperate game with the Romanian government, until finally, no matter from what country we mailed the Bibles, nearly every one would be returned.

Because of the increasing pressure of the Romanian government against Christians, we were also running out of names and addresses. Desperate as they were for Bibles, few believers dared to risk the consequences attendant upon having this forbidden "propaganda" openly sent through the mail to their homes. Suddenly we found ourselves faced with a dilemma: Money was being received designated for Bibles to Romania, but we were no longer able to get them to the thousands of believers in that country who had never possessed one of their own.

We were slowly learning from our mistakes. Not only did the method we had been using place the recipient of a Bible in an awkward, and sometimes even dangerous, position, but it was also a very costly method both in terms of postage, wrapping paper, string, and the time it took to package and address all of this mail. Furthermore, we had begun to long for a closer contact with the Christians themselves. Even if it had been possible to communicate freely by mail, that could never take the place of meeting them face-to-face. A conviction had been growing within me that such meetings were not only desirable for purposes of communication and bringing aid, but absolutely essential if we were to realize in practice the truth of the oneness of the body of Christ throughout the world. No barrier should be allowed to separate the children of God in the East from those in the West.

By this time I had also learned that the situation in Romania was not unique. Bulgaria and Russia were probably even worse.

I used to cry out to God day and night, "Lord, what can we do? We cannot use the traditional methods any longer!"

On my knees one day, as I was repeating this prayer, it seemed to me that I heard the Spirit of the Lord respond:

"I am not the God of tradition. I am the God of life!"

In my mind I saw a river flowing deep and strong. A landslide had blocked its path, but the force of the current could not be contained. Sweeping around the obstruction, the river found a new way to reach its destination by forging a new channel in earth and rock.

This revelation made an impression upon me so profound that it affected my entire approach to Christian service ever after. In my heart I knew with deep assurance that God was saying: "If you walk with Me, you will discover that there are always new ways of life, and I will show you things that you never thought were possible."

From that moment I began to seek for other methods to get Bibles into the East and also to transmit funds to the many believers in Communist countries who, because of special government sanctions against them for their faith, were living in poverty.

In those early days I had not yet met Brother Andrew nor the many others working in the East; nor was I aware of the means others were using. We prayed, asking God to guide us, and we concluded, as the early Christians had before us, that we ought to obey God rather than men. This would be our rule of conduct in all things. Where we could do God's will without violating human laws we would. But whenever a government, capitalist or Communist, sought to impose laws that, if obeyed, would cause us to disobey our Lord's commands, our duty was clear, and so would be our consciences.

This was the principle upon which our work in Eastern Europe began.

In the years that followed, it had been my task (as the founder of the mission) to develop contacts in Communist countries with believers who could help pass on Bibles to those who needed them. During my trips into the East, I also sought to discover or verify the identity of pastors and families of prisoners and martyrs who were in financial need so we could aid them with available funds.

Our mission had been working for years in other countries of Eastern Europe. This, my first trip into Russia, had been undertaken for the purpose of extending our work to that land, also.

Lying in that hotel room in Brest the night of our arrest, I retraced the intervening years to ponder my metamorphosis from pastor to "spy, thief, and robber" as I now stood accused. I went carefully over every step that had led me into a ministry behind the Iron Curtain—and now into the custody of the Soviets. And I asked myself, and the Lord, if I had gone astray somewhere, gotten out of His will, started following my plans instead of His.

Was my present predicament my own fault? Not really an abuse I was suffering for the cause of Christ, but an ill-fated adventure of my own making?

Was it wrong to hide the Bibles?

When they had taken the car apart with their tools, the guards had looked everywhere—except the one place where the Bibles were. That wasn't due to my cleverness. Wasn't it really God who had kept them from finding the Bibles? Then why had they found those three beside the road? If God had preserved them at the border, why hadn't they gotten to the villages where they were needed?

Couldn't I trust God, even for the Bibles they had found?

As to wrongdoing, my accusers had been unable to cite even one law that I had broken. My conscience was clear on that. And even if there had been a law against bringing Bibles, I was now more convinced than ever that it would be an abomination to God to obey it. I had done the right thing, of that I was sure, no matter what the consequences.

But the consequences did matter. There was a tightness in my throat whenever I let my thoughts settle on that subject. I had always carried myself with the air of a man willing to be a martyr for Christ, if necessary. Now I concentrated my attention on those two significant words—*if necessary.*

In the process of pondering what they really meant, I discovered that I was afraid.

3

The Cost of Obedience

Bent and I awakened early following a restless and troubled sleep. After washing and dressing, we read our Bibles and prayed together, committing ourselves and our loved ones at home into God's care. Under house arrest in that old hotel, looking out over the city of Brest going about its business below us, cut off from all contact with the outside world and waiting for our interrogators to appear, the seriousness of our predicament began to impress itself upon us more fully. How long would it be before our families would become worried and attempt to trace our movements? We tried to tell ourselves that we would soon be released, yet at the same time feared that we wouldn't. Calling upon God to give us the strength to face whatever might be His will, we had too many heavy concerns to feel hungry.

It was nearing 10:30 A.M. when finally there was a quick knock, and before we could answer, the door was pushed open. Four men and a woman stepped into the small room. They were obviously a team of specialists who had come some distance to question us. Their professional competence was quickly apparent.

"You are Kristian?" asked an intelligent-looking young man of about thirty, his dark blond hair close-cropped in typical Russian style. The voice was friendly, the look open and direct. The approach was a far cry from yesterday's explosive exchange at the border.

I nodded my acknowledgment.

"I am your interpreter," explained the young man, extending his hand, but without offering to give me his name. His English was far better than mine.

Shaking hands next with Bent, he said, "You will go with them." He gestured toward a tall, slim woman dressed in rather mannish clothes, and a graying, heavy-set man wearing a shabby, tieless suit.

"We have another room down the hall," said the woman, beckoning for Bent to follow. Her English was impeccable.

"Sit down and relax," I was told through my interpreter by the man who was apparently going to question me. He was about sixty, plumpish and wide jowled. His quick eyes assessed me and the room almost instantaneously, then settled into a narrow squint that I suspected was meant to be a friendly smile, but only accented the shrewd expression into which his face seemed to have frozen.

The fourth man in the group, who remained for the moment listening intently, seemed to be in charge. He was in and out of the room constantly and appeared to be coordinating the questioning, depending upon the answers Bent and I each gave. About forty, his sharp features and steely eyes topped a huge frame. I found it easy to picture him as a basketball player, or even as a champion discus or javelin thrower in bygone days, but he was very much overweight now.

At first I was asked only such innocuous questions as how I liked Russia, how long I had been there, if I had visited it before, and why I had come. Then my questioner reminded me that I was under arrest for bringing Bibles into the country, and asked if that was true. Had I really brought Bibles into Russia?

I readily admitted that.

"Didn't you know that is forbidden?" he asked.

"I'm not aware of any law against bringing Bibles as gifts," I replied.

He had apparently been informed of my arguments about the legality of what I had done, so didn't pursue that point. In fact the way he dropped it, moving on to something else, made me realize that my fate did not depend upon questions of law but solely their will. I was completely at their mercy.

"You pretended to come as a tourist," he continued quickly. "You should have been a real tourist and then you would have had no trouble. In fact, you hid your intentions just as you hid your Bibles. Like an enemy spy, you didn't tell us that you were a Christian bringing harmful propaganda to our people."

"That's not true," I objected. "At the border where we entered I told the Intourist interpreter—the very first Russian I met—that I was a Christian, and talked to him about God."

He raised his eyebrows in surprise. "We don't have this information. What did you say?"

"I asked if he believed in God, and he said that he didn't believe in things he couldn't understand. 'Do you believe the universe is without end?' I asked him. He said, 'Yes, otherwise we would have to ask what lies beyond it.' So I asked him if he could understand that, and he admitted that he couldn't. Then he said he was too scientific to believe in something he couldn't see, and I told him of things he couldn't see but believed in. You cannot be a true scientist and not believe in God. So you see, I did not hide my intentions like a spy!"

He had opened his mouth as though to stop me, but I

had kept right on talking. Now he was frowning. "It is
forbidden to speak about God like that in the Soviet
Union," he admonished me. "For our own citizens,
religious propaganda must be confined to licensed
churches only. And for visitors like you it is forbidden
entirely."

"But Christ has told us to go into all the world and to
tell everyone everywhere that He died for their sins. We
Christians will continue to obey Him even if you forbid
us!"

"Then you must suffer the consequences," he said
sharply, dropping any pretence at friendliness. "Certainly
you know that you have defied our laws and committed
a very serious crime. Unless I recommend leniency for
cooperation, you will probably receive a sentence of ten
years!"

I drew in my breath sharply, and my heart began to
pound so loudly that I was sure they could both hear it.
Ten years! Was he just bluffing? The day before I would
have been sure it was a bluff, but now I didn't know.
Obviously I had underestimated the seriousness of our
situation. But ten years!

He was watching me carefully, and I knew that my
reaction had not passed unnoticed. I was angry with
myself for having betrayed my fear, and determined to
regain the ground I had just lost.

"There are millions of Christians in the West," I said
firmly, trying to keep my voice from quavering. "What
good will it do to put two of us in prison? Even if you
write a law against it, we will still bring Bibles because
you have no right to prevent Christians from having their
handbook!"

"Your country would not allow me to bring Communist
propaganda to its citizens, would it?" he exclaimed
indignantly. The expression on his face told me that he
believed this and that he was sincere in his accusation

against me. I really had committed a great crime, to his way of thinking.

"Bring all the Communist literature you wish," I replied, feeling suddenly that I could reason with him, now that I understood his thinking a little better. "You may shout your slogans along the streets, advertise your beliefs in the newspapers, publish your literature in Denmark—all of it you wish!"

There was a look of disbelief on his face. "And the censors? I suppose they would just accept this?" The tone was scornful, as though to warn me that he knew I was lying.

"Censors?" I asked in genuine surprise. "What are they? We don't have such people in Denmark. Ours is a free country. We're not afraid of your propaganda. Everyone has the right to state his opinion and to believe as he pleases in Denmark!" I wished I could express to him by contrast the oppression I felt in his country, an oppression that had caused me the night before to take that Russian New Testament from under my shirt and hide it beneath a mattress, but I didn't dare.

A confused expression had crept over his face, as though he were on the verge of believing me. Then, in an instant, the mask was back in place, and he changed the subject.

Suddenly I was depressed by the feeling that we could never communicate. He could never believe me—we lived in two different worlds. My mind was reeling with the possibility of prison. Yesterday I wouldn't have taken it seriously, but now I believed him. It was a battle to keep my face from betraying the fear that was draining my strength and leaving me feeling limp and nauseated.

"You have a state church in Denmark," he said, "so you're not free as you tried to tell me you are. In Russia we have separation of church and state under our constitution."

"Doesn't the church have to be licensed by the government in Russia?" I asked.

"Of course," he replied.

"Then how can you say the church is separate from the state? We have many churches besides the state church in Denmark. But even our state church is free—to meet when and where the members please, to preach what they believe is God's will, to choose their pastors. The state interferes in none of this. But in your country your government controls the church, shuts churches down, imprisons church officials, tells the pastors what to preach, won't let the Christians talk about God or worship Him except in a church building—yet you call this separation of church and state?"

He looked uncomfortable and the interpreter seemed shocked at my boldness.

"We print Bibles in Russia: Why did you want to bring more into our country?" he demanded.

"Because there are thousands of Christians in the Soviet Union who can't get Bibles. Your government only prints a handful. Christ said that man shall not live by bread alone but by every word that proceeds out of the mouth of God. The Bible is the Word of God, and all men need it for life, if they are to be more than animals."

I was now determined that if I were going to prison, at least I would do my utmost to take these two men to heaven on the way.

A long series of questions followed, involving where I had gotten the Bibles, who prints Russian Bibles in the West, how many Bible societies there are, whether they coordinate their efforts, how they are financed, who directs them. I answered each question truthfully, based upon the limited information that I had. They apparently had not associated our mission's stationery in Bent's Bible with either of us. If they discovered that I was the head of a mission, I knew it would be much worse for me.

About 2:00 P.M. the tall, heavy man pushed open the door and said something from the hallway. My questioner and the interpreter stood to their feet wearily.

"We're going to give you an hour to write down everything we've talked about," I was told. Putting some paper and a pencil on a small table near the door, they left me alone.

I assumed that they were going out for lunch and had left me this assignment to keep me from resting. But I didn't intend to oblige them. I resented the thought of their relaxing over a meal and drinks in a restaurant, while I was getting dizzy from hunger and my thirst was becoming unbearable. Most of that hour I spent reading my Bible and praying. The last few minutes I used up the paper they had left by writing a brief summary in a very large scrawl.

Returning from lunch looking rested and well fed, my interrogator began to ask many questions about radio broadcasts. It soon became apparent that the great number of Russians listening to Christian radio programs, and their effectiveness in spite of jamming, was a cause of serious concern to the Soviet authorities. I was impressed again with his sincerity as he denounced the dishonest tactics of beaming "propaganda harmful to the system" into the homes of Soviet citizens and thereby undoing years of careful atheistic indoctrination. The expression on his face was so intent and the tone of his voice so earnest as he questioned me that I began to understand as never before the effectiveness of Christian radio broadcasts to Russia—and the Soviet objection to them as unfair outside opposition directed against the very foundations of Marxist-Leninist society. He could not understand any attempt to persuade men to believe in Christ except as an attack upon the Communist system, which according to him would only work when everyone was an atheist.

My interrogator now concentrated upon what I soon realized was a major objective—the identity of those to whom we had given Bibles. He seemed especially anxious to know if anyone had received more than one. Again and again he came back to the question of how many Bibles we had given to each person. The tall, fat man was going back and forth between Bent's room and mine, looking quite disturbed. Finally I remembered Bent telling me on the street the night before that he had disclosed at the customs office that we had given ten Bibles to one man. My failure to verify this was apparently considered to be a serious discrepancy.

"I do remember that we gave ten Bibles to someone," I said at last, as soon as I suspected that this was what they were waiting to hear. There was a momentary relaxation of expression on the face of my questioner as though finally he was making progress.

"This man's identity is of the utmost importance to us," he said solemnly. Leaning closer to me, his voice took on a confidential, even solicitous tone. "I'm sure the judge, at my recommendation, would consider reducing your sentence substantially if you cooperate with our investigation. Do you remember this man's name?"

"I'm not sure he even told me his name," I replied thoughtfully as though I were trying hard to remember.

"Where did you meet him?"

"In Minsk, I believe."

"Where in Minsk?"

"I don't remember exactly."

"Describe the man. It's extremely important for both of us."

On and on the questions went, my interrogator determined to extract this man's identity from me, and I equally determined not to betray him. I had promised myself I would rather die than do that. I could never forget this man, the light that came into his eyes when he saw the Bibles, the tears that ran down his cheeks, the way he embraced us, the divine love we shared as brothers in Christ, and the overflowing joy that made us laugh together in spite of the fact that our rendezvous had to be secret and brief. Just to meet him had been an experience that would live in my heart forever. Successfully, I avoided giving an answer that would betray him.

At about six o'clock my interrogator looked at his watch and stood to his feet with a yawn. Apparently they were going to take another break, perhaps even eat supper. But I was not to be allowed any rest.

"You will have one hour," he said through the interpreter, "to write down a full and accurate account of everything you've done since entering the Soviet Union. We want to know exactly where you went, with whom you spoke, to whom you gave each Bible—everything."

He pulled several sheets of cheap yellow paper from his briefcase and dropped them on the small table beside the door as he left.

Alone, I looked at my watch and decided to spend forty-five minutes in Bible study and prayer, saving the last fifteen minutes to write my report, which I knew would be brief. Assuming that Bent had been left to do the same thing, I hoped that our meticulous investigators wouldn't find some fine discrepancy between our accounts to form the basis of further detailed questioning. Already that was beginning to wear on me. How much longer would they keep it up without at least giving me something to ease the thirst flaming in my throat?

I opened my Bible, but there was no use trying to read. My mind was far away in Denmark, with Ninna and the children. My eyes filled with tears. I could see Ninna, just the way she had looked when first I noticed her, and my thoughts drifted back to that special day.

I had been an elder in a small church, doing most of

the preaching because the pastor was advanced in years. This particular Sunday I noticed a new girl singing in the choir. She had such laughing eyes and her face seemed to be expressing what the words of each song meant to her. From that day on I loved to watch her sing, but had no idea that my interest went any deeper, until one Sunday she wasn't there, and I felt a strangely bittersweet emptiness inside. Inquiring, I learned that she had gone away on vacation. When she returned two weeks later, I asked her if I could talk with her. We had never really spoken more than a passing word.

Driving slowly through the streets of Copenhagen, I groped for words to express what was in my heart. I had always been too busy serving my Saviour to have time for dating girls, but I had known that when God's time came He would show me His choice for my life. Now He had told me plainly that Ninna was the one.

Sitting by the hotel window looking out over the city of Brest, I could hear myself saying, ''Ninna, I believe the Lord has chosen us for each other. Do you also think so?'' I could see again the quick blush in her cheeks, hear her gasp, and then her face had broken into a radiant smile. She was nodding, and those expressive eyes were telling me that God had already said the same thing to her.

Scenes of our simple wedding flashed before me. And our children—two boys and a girl—chubby, pink-cheeked babies in Ninna's arms, then learning to walk, to talk. How quickly they had grown. The eldest was already eight years old.

I turned from the window and wept at the thought of going to prison and being without them! I could never bear that! It made me feel ashamed to admit it, but it was true. I was no hero. But wasn't this love? Should I be ashamed of the love that God had given me for them—or was it really fear for my own fate that pained me most deeply? How could I know my own heart?

Falling on my knees beside the bed, I sobbed out my

confusion, telling the Lord how much I loved them, admitting that I was afraid for myself, asking Him for strength. But the torment I felt only increased. It seemed that God was asking, "How much do you love *Me?* Are you willing to be cut off from all you love, if this is My will for your life?"

To be cut off from *all* I loved? That question gave me new insights. Suddenly I could see a whole procession of things I loved very much. The apartment that we had moved into not so long before. It was just what we had wanted, but I had never known that I loved it. Was that true? And the roses in the garden—yes, I loved the roses very much. They meant more to me than I had realized. To be without them would make prison that much harder to bear. I could no longer water and fertilize, prune and clip them, nor bring in a fragrant bouquet to Ninna and watch her put them into a vase to display their beauty and spread their aroma throughout our happy home.

And the books. I loved them, too, the hundreds of volumes that lined the many shelves. I loved the thought of being able to show them to visitors, to pick up any one of them at any time and lean back in my special chair and glance over familiar pages. I was even proud of my books—but in prison I would be without them.

And I loved being a pastor. Perhaps that was why I wasn't the father and the husband I ought to be—I loved so many other things that I often didn't have time for those I loved the most, Ninna and the children. My first duty was neglected while I ran in pursuit of others. I was often angry with them, too. Even after preaching about being under the control of the Holy Spirit, my temper would get out of control. Yes, especially when I had preached about that. What was the good of knowing something in my head if I couldn't live it in my life?

"That's just the way it is with me right now!" I sobbed the words out to the Lord. "I have preached about surrender to Your will, but I confess that I'm not willing to go to prison. I'm not willing to give up my wife and the children, not even the roses and books. I have told You before: Not my will but Thine be done—but I have said it with my lips, not with my heart. I can only say it that way now. I come to You and ask You to make me be really willing from my heart to do Your will, whatever it is."

I gave up trying to pray and trying to surrender. Not only would God have to provide the strength to carry me through prison, but He would have to give me the strength to be willing to accept it from His hand.

Now that I had quit talking to Him, He began speaking to me. The verse flashed into my mind: Who for the joy set before Him endured the cross. That was the secret. I had wanted to surrender to His will as a hero—but God didn't ask me to be a hero. He only asked me to believe that His will was best, that the reward He would give in exchange would be far greater than anything I would be called upon to sacrifice.

Suddenly I knew as clearly as I knew my own existence in God's creation that I *wanted* His will. To miss that would be to miss life itself. All else was death, no matter how attractively packaged. To choose His will was no hero's sacrifice, but faith's acceptance of that which infinite love and wisdom had decided was best for me. And if that meant to be in prison, then that was where I wanted above all else to be—in His will.

Rising from my knees, I sat on the edge of the bed and reached for my Bible. It was open at Isaiah 50. Reading hungrily, I came to those words in chapter 51:7-16: "Fear ye not the reproach of men, neither be ye afraid of their revilings...the redeemed of the Lord shall return, and come with singing unto Zion; and everlasting joy shall be upon their head: they shall obtain gladness and joy; and sorrow and mourning shall flee away. I...am he that comforteth you: who art thou, that thou shouldest be afraid of...the son of man which shall be made as grass;

And forgettest the Lord. . . and hast feared continually. . . because of the fury of the oppressor. . . ? The captive exile hasteneth that he may be loosed. . . [that his spirit should not fail]. . . I have put my words in thy mouth, and I have covered thee in the shadow of my hand. . . . ''

Isaiah had penned that prophecy almost 3,000 years before, but in my heart I knew that in some mysterious way it was God's promise to me at that very moment. The thought was not wishful thinking, a vain hope, a straw that I was grasping at in desperation—but something I *knew*. A few moments before I had been in despair, gripped by the fear of languishing in prison, and now I knew with absolute certainty that I would be set free. The living God, the Maker of heaven and earth, had communicated this assurance to my heart.

I wept again, but now it was for joy.

Suddenly I realized that the hour had almost ended. Sitting down at the table, I hurriedly wrote a brief summary of my movements within Russia since we had arrived.

When my interrogation began again, I had a new strength. With greater boldness I made my answer to each question a framework for sharing Christ. Under arrest for bringing Bibles into Russia, I quoted the Bible as often as I could think of a verse that would fit the answer I was giving.

Finally, in exasperation, my investigator demanded, "Why do you always give replies from the Bible?"

"This is God's Word that brings life to all who believe it," I replied. "I came to Russia to give it to your people. I also want to give it to you, so that you may have eternal life. I want you to know the Christ who lives in my heart!"

Neither my investigator nor the man in charge who coordinated the questioning seemed to have any interest in what I tried to share of Christ from Scriptures, but I noticed that the interpreter was drinking in the Word of God like a man who had suddenly come upon a clear, cool stream in the middle of the desert. Later in the evening, when my interrogator seemed to tire and there were long pauses between questions, I began to tell the interpreter more about Christ. I sensed that his heart was opening.

Leaving orders to be ready for more questioning early in the morning, the team finally left late that night. Bent and I rushed to the railway station just before it closed to quench our thirst and get something to eat.

"I think they're going too far," said Bent as we stood together at a counter in the crowded station restaurant, comparing notes quietly in Danish.

"What do you mean?" I asked. "They can do anything they want. This is Russia!"

"Russia or not," said Bent, "I know from my experience in the military that they've gone beyond the Geneva Convention. They grilled me for two hours just about radio programs beaming into Russia. They have no right to ask us all these questions about organizations in the West. We should demand our rights to contact our embassy!"

Crawling into bed an hour later, after Bent and I had sung hymns and prayed together, I remembered that in 1960 the Baptist church in this very town of Brest had lost its license because its members were critical of new regulations suspending baptism for young people under eighteen and restraining "unhealthy missionary tendencies." Deprived of a place in which to worship together, the congregation of nearly four hundred members had refused to go out of existence. Because of this, the two leaders, Trofim Feidak and Vladimir Vilchinisky, had been sentenced to five years in prison. After their imprisonment, Mihail Bartoshuk had courageously taken up the leadership of this "illegal" congregation. He, too, had been arrested and sentenced to five years in a strict labor camp.

My mind was full of the names of such men and women

paying the price of obedience to God all over Russia. To become a fellow prisoner with them would be a privilege. The eternal reward Christ offered in exchange would be far greater than any temporary loss I might suffer. Understanding this—and being willing at last—brought as much peace and joy to my heart as had the promise from Isaiah that we would be set free.

4

A Blessing in Disguise

When the investigation team arrived about 7:00 the next morning, Bent and I were ready for them, having agreed upon what we would say. This time we made sure the door was locked. After they had knocked twice, I opened the door halfway and stood there with my hand on the knob, blocking their entrance.

"You have kept us incommunicado for two days," I announced firmly, making no move to let them in. "We have committed no crime—you have not named one law that we have broken—yet you have treated us as criminals!"

Instead of the angry reaction I had expected, the tall man in charge plucked at his cheek nervously. There was an uneasy shuffling of feet and clearing of throats from the rest of the team.

"If you don't release us within one hour," I continued righteously, feeling a growing boldness, "we won't answer another question until we've talked to the Danish Embassy in Moscow. You've violated the Geneva Convention! We're going to report this to our authorities!"

They withdrew a few steps down the hall and consulted

among themselves in low whispers. When they returned
to the doorway, my interpreter announced: "There are
only a few more questions to ask. It won't take over an
hour. Then you'll be released."

I saw the leader start down the stairs. "This is too big
a decision for him," I thought. "They're stalling us while
he calls someone higher up for orders."

Bent was led off as usual to another room and I was
left with my half of the team. My interrogator began by
rewording some of the same questions he had been
working on late the night before, but there was no life
in his voice. He seemed to have lost interest in my case.

After a few halfhearted probes, he fell into silence.

"If you have nothing further to ask, then I'd like to tell
you more about why I came," I said, and began to explain
how I wanted the Russian people, including these two
men, to know the true God who created us all and to
experience forgiveness and eternal life in Jesus Christ, the
crucified and resurrected Saviour.

The interpreter faithfully translated everything I said
into Russian, but the interrogator was obviously unin-
terested. He drummed his fingers impatiently on his
knees, then stood up and began to pace the small room
restlessly, pausing now and then in front of the window
to look out over Brest. His thoughts were apparently miles
away.

Left to ourselves, the interpreter began to ask me
thoughtful questions, betraying an eagerness to hear more
about Christ that startled me. Lowering our voices, we
talked together in English quietly and earnestly, leaving
the interrogator to his own thoughts. The young Russian
hitched forward on the edge of the bed facing me,
absorbed in what I was telling him about Christ. A look
of enlightenment was coming into his face. It was obvious
that the seed of God's Word was falling on fertile ground.

I had taken the New Testament from under the mattress early that morning and returned it to my coat pocket.

As the interpreter continued eagerly questioning me about Christ, I wanted to give the Testament to him—but I was afraid. The thought crossed my mind: "Suppose he isn't really interested—what if this is just a ploy to get me to give away some information?" But he was only asking about Christ and God, the Bible, heaven and hell.

The interrogator was standing in front of the window with his back to us, looking down on the city. Now was my chance. Putting my hand into the pocket, I held the small book in my fingers, struggling with myself. Suppose the investigator turned around just at the wrong moment—or what if my interpreter were afraid to accept it?

No, I was the one who was afraid, and it didn't make sense. They knew that I had given away Bibles. One more would make no difference, and this young Russian was so eager to learn, so hungry for the Word of God.

While I hesitated, still afraid, the interrogator turned away from the window and slumped into a chair by the small table, watching us curiously. I had lost my opportunity, and a wave of self-condemnation swept over me. Perhaps there would be another chance, and then. . .

Suddenly the door burst open and the group leader stepped back into the room. Through the open doorway I could see Bent coming down the hall behind him.

"The hour is up and you're going to be released," he exclaimed, sounding glad to be done with this assignment. "Get your things and come with us."

That New Testament felt like a lead weight in my pocket as we walked down the stairs to the lobby, carrying our half-empty suitcases.

Bent and I both thought that the Soviet government should pay for our hotel room. Mumbling something in Danish about being "a guest of the government," a phrase I had often heard used in connection with prison and arrest, I told Bent it was a misnomer, at least in Russia. But we didn't argue the point. Paying the bill, we happily checked out of the hotel, and walked through the empty lobby to the street outside, where we were told, to our surprise, that the investigating team had no car and would we mind if three of them rode with us?

Appearing to be in good humor for the first time, the tall, overweight ex-athlete, whose huge hulk seemed to dwarf our small vehicle, laughingly suggested that the only way would be for him to ride on the roof. In my mind I could see the car flattened to the pavement. Somehow we managed to squeeze him into the backseat beside my interpreter and interrogator, and we set off for the border with the rear bumper only a few inches off the street.

The drive back to the customs office was like a scene from a comic opera. The Russians joked good-naturedly with us, and that mountain of a man shook the whole car when he laughed. Our former antagonists were trying so hard to be friendly that one would almost have thought we were a group of old friends riding to the office together.

Now that most of the tension was gone, it surprised me to discover that I really had a warm feeling toward these men. Though our views were still poles apart, we had begun to respect one another's sincerity. Beneath their atheistic ideology, which I detested, I had found human beings whom I could love. It was a beautiful experience, but at the same time tinged with sadness. I found my joy at the prospect of release strangely tarnished by the feeling that I would miss these men and the friendship we might have known together. We would be separated not just by distance, but by a system that allowed them no freedom to examine alternate points of view.

This realization prompted me to remind Bent that we weren't out yet and that we should pray continuously until we actually crossed into Poland.

I parked the car in front of the main customs office, and we all went inside. Bent and I were told to sit on a bench and wait. The small building was already crowded beyond its capacity with officials and newspaper journalists, and more continued to arrive. Finally, after we had been waiting for nearly two hours, a small police car pulled up in front and the same tall, red-faced man who had been in charge before climbed out and hurried inside, looking harassed but important. He impressed me as being perpetually behind schedule. Eyeing us unpleasantly, he motioned us to join him in some chairs placed in front of a low table. Reporters were beginning to take seats on the other side.

Standing to our feet, we both noticed for the first time the large motion-picture camera that was now being maneuvered into position.

"Looks as though we're going to be on television, or on a newsreel," Bent whispered.

"No matter what we say in this interview," I whispered back, "they'll make it come out the way they want it to. But there's one thing they can't change—that's the expression on our faces. Whatever happens, keep smiling. Let the love of Christ really come through, so the Russian people will know we're not the kind of monsters the official interpretation is going to say we are."

Sitting down in front of the low table, we noticed that it was covered with exhibits—Christian literature, the three Bibles they had recovered, some ball-point pens, and several nylon shirts we had taken with us to give away because they're all very hard to get in Eastern Europe.

What followed was not really an interview but a performance. The Great Angry One, who had apparently written the script, directed the show. Like an overheated volcano, he erupted at almost predictable intervals, spewing righteous indignation upon our heads, not forgetting to face the camera for special emphasis on major points. I felt more like an observer than a participant, watching him address the Russian people via the corrective lectures he was ostensibly making to me and Bent,

including the virtues of atheism, the unscientific back-
wardness and reactionary nature of all Christians, the
cowardice of spies, and the undeniable link between
capitalism, imperialism, and the deceptive myths promul-
gated by preachers of Christianity. Nor did he forget to
gush ebullient praise for the honest and vigilant Soviet
citizen who had reported us to the authorities.

In between a running explanation for the television
audience, Bent and I were led back over familiar ground.
We had brought forbidden literature, harmful to the
system, within the Soviet borders. (There were expressions of shock, then rapid writing of notes by the journalists.) Like spies, we had disguised our intentions,
pretending to be honest tourists, and had cleverly hidden
the harmful propaganda. (Gasps of shocked amazement
at our audacity, then more quick writing of notes.) We
had been apprehended through the vigilance of honest
citizens who refused our poisonous, imperialist propaganda. (Quick scribbling—a good point!) Any other
citizens who had been deceived into accepting Bibles as
gifts were called upon to come forward immediately and
rid their consciences (heads nodded, the writing quickened) of all implication in this international plot (gasps)
and join hands with all Soviet citizens in stemming this
tide of religious literature preaching seductive myths that
had been flooding (flooding?—fast writing, that *was* news!)
into Russia because of its generous open-border policy.

After summarizing his case, the Great Angry One
demanded that we confess our crime. Even if it meant
that we would not be released after all, I couldn't con-
sent to that.

"We have broken no laws," I said to the journalists and
camera. "I will tell you frankly that we brought Bibles
into Russia—but since your constitution guarantees freedom of religion, then every citizen must have the right
to possess the Christian handbook if he wishes. We

brought the Bibles because Christ has commanded us to
go...."

He cut me off. "*Now* you admit what you did—but you
didn't admit this when you entered our country. You hid
the Bibles and your intention then! If you thought what
you were doing was not against the law, then why did
you hide the Bibles?"

"You silly fellow," I thought to myself. "You should
know better than to ask that question—or perhaps your
subordinate didn't tell you...."

Turning to face the audience again, I opened my coat
and pulled out my wallet. "None of you would deny that
it is lawful to carry money," I said, opening the wallet
and displaying some bills. "Yet I also hide my money in
my coat like this..." Here I returned it to my pocket.
"...because if I don't, there are thieves and robbers just
waiting for the chance to take it away from me!" I
gestured toward the Bibles on the table to illustrate my
point.

I had expected a few suppressed titters, but instead, as
soon as my interpreter, struggling to keep a straight face,
had faithfully given the translation, the journalists, camera crew, and even some of the officials standing in the
rear burst into loud, appreciative laughter. The Great
Angry One glared around the room in absolute fury,
which only seemed to heighten the sense of the ridiculous, and the rolling laughter swelled to such a roar that
I felt sorry for him.

When the laughter had subsided to a reverent silence,
and pencils were once more poised, the Great Angry One
tried to carry on as before, but there was a different
atmosphere in the room. All over his audience repentant
expressions alternated on the same faces with furtive
smiles hidden behind hands and paper. There was now
a general air of restlessness punctuated by nervous coughs
that one might suspect were a cover for irrepressible

recurrences of laughter. The momentum and drama he had built up was no longer there.

After a brief reminder to everyone that we were dangerous criminals, we were told that leniency was being extended to us as an example of goodwill—although we well deserved a prison sentence—and we were to be released. All of our personal belongings would be returned to us; however, the Bibles, literature, and all films we had taken were being confiscated.

Waves of disappointment swept over me. "Oh, Lord!" I prayed silently. "I thought You had promised to save those films. They're so important!"

Then my conscience smote me for being ungrateful. "Thank You, Lord, for setting us free. Thank You, Lord! Thank You!"

We gathered into our arms the two small piles of personal belongings being returned to us; then the camera crew and journalists followed us out to our car. With that crowd around us, watching our every move, the camera going, it was difficult not to feel like condemned criminals who were being granted an undeserved amnesty. I felt so many eyes staring at me, some hostile, some in pity, and others in disdain. I felt an impulse to hang my head, to cover my face with my hands, to run and hide somewhere, and I knew Bent must be feeling the same way.

"Keep your head up and keep smiling," I said to Bent loudly in Danish, as much to remind myself as him. "And keep praying. We haven't been given our passports yet!"

Looking around, I could see that the border had been sealed off. Cars were lined up waiting to cross into Poland, but were being kept at a distance until we had been processed.

We climbed into our auto. Following orders, I turned the car around and drove back toward Brest, past the line of cars waiting behind the barrier. About half a mile from the customs office, we were stopped and the three Russian Bibles were handed back to Bent. Then we were given careful instructions; I was to drive the car slowly toward the camera crew stationed just ahead of us, while Bent was to throw the Bibles wrapped in plastic one at a time from the window onto the grassy shoulder beside the road. Perhaps the Russian television audience would be told that we had been photographed by the alert Soviet police in the very act.

The questioning look Bent gave me said, "What kind of a charade is this?"

I whispered back, "Why not? Let whoever watches this film know that Christians come from the West to bring Bibles into Russia—and give them a big smile!"

We couldn't help smiling, it seemed too ludicrous, especially when the cameraman had my interpreter ask us to back up the car and do it again. The Bibles were hastily gathered from the roadside by an official and handed back to us.

"Maybe they're auditioning us for lead roles in a spy movie," I quipped.

I drove slowly forward, and Bent dropped the Bibles into the grass once more. He wasn't only smiling, but laughing this time. We both loved it, and the camera crew seemed happy with our performance.

Looking like a Hollywood production company on location, our entourage of director, assistant directors, camera crew, sound engineer, actors, and extras drove back again, bypassing the line of cars at the barrier. This time we proceeded on past the customs buildings toward Poland. Our car was stopped in the center of the narrow road just where the approach meets the bridge over the River Bug, which marks the Russian-Polish border at this point. We were both ordered to get out and stand in front of our auto.

The Great Angry One, who had been directing the entire proceedings like a Russian Cecil B. DeMille, walked stiffly up to me and with a pompous flourish extended a hand holding my passport. The camera was going full tilt at close range.

"Here is your passport," he said haughtily. "You have come to our country like a thief and a robber, and you are no longer welcome. We welcome tourists, but we don't welcome people like you. You must never come back!"

My interpreter from the hotel, who had so eagerly asked me questions about Christ a few hours before, had been the official translator during all of these proceedings. I had seen respect, even love in his face, and felt a bond growing between us during the "press conference." We were facing one another now for the last time. As he gave the translation of these final words being spoken to me, there were tears in his eyes. His lips trembled with suppressed emotion.

"*He* says you came like thieves and robbers," said my interpreter to me softly in English, "but *I* don't say so."

Our eyes met briefly. . . and the look he gave me told me that he had become a brother in Christ.

I felt an impulse to hug him, to say something encouraging, to cry, to shout at the camera that the love we felt for one another, this love that pierced borders, that dissolved hatred and misunderstanding, was my only mission and the one message of the Book I had brought into Russia.

With an effort I turned my attention back to the Great Angry One and took the passport he was holding out to me.

It was like a wide-awake dream. I was choked with emotion. A new babe had been born into God's family, but I couldn't speak to him, didn't dare to give him the New Testament that burned in my pocket. That was forbidden propaganda, harmful to the system. My face must betray nothing, neither the elation I felt at the triumph of one soul, nor the sorrow at the rejection of Christ by so many others.

I could hear the sound of the camera whirring in my ears and sense the presence of the others, but for a moment time stood still. Turning, I looked back into Russia. From my elevated vantage point on the bridge I could see reporters and officials standing in loose clusters in front of the customs buildings watching us. More cars were lined up now outside the barrier. Beyond lay Brest with all its memories for me, and its present troubles for a congregation meeting in secret, its leaders imprisoned.

"What a farce!" I thought. "So many words, but what does it all mean? What is this game we're playing? Why are they so determined to stamp out all belief in God? Not long ago they threatened me with prison. Now I'm leaving and I think they are the ones who are in prison."

I felt so small and helpless, an insignificant and uncomprehending creature sucked into a whirling maelstrom of events that seemed unreal. I felt detached from life as I once thought I knew it. A montage of scenes and impressions from the past few days flashed before me: Bibles, tears, smiles, embraces, the Great Angry One, my investigator, the interpreter, the hotel room, prayer, questions, answers, questions, threats, evasion, anger, fear, hiding the New Testament, confession, suspicion, trust. The war was not really between Christians and Communists. We were mere flesh and blood, but the real antagonists were locked in bitter combat in another world. Our struggles with ourselves and with one another were like shadows falling across the earth projected by spiritual beings fighting in a battle between God and Satan.

For a moment I caught a glimpse of that battlefield and heard the sound of mysterious weapons. A veil had been drawn aside. I could almost touch and see a reality in another dimension. I struggled to understand, almost grasped the ungraspable . . . when the interpreter's voice translating for the Great Angry One brought me back to the three-dimensional world of a bridge spanning the River Bug between Russia and Poland.

"Here is your passport, also. Next time you come to Russia, don't come with Mr. Hans—bring your wife."

Bent took his passport. We climbed back into our car and drove across the bridge into Poland. I looked in the rearview mirror to catch one last glimpse of my new brother. He and the Great Angry One were walking side by side just behind the camera crew. Beyond, the barrier had been raised and a line of cars was moving slowly toward the customs buildings.

A small contingent of broadly smiling Polish officers was waiting for us.

"Good afternoon, gentlemen," said one of them, taking the passports I offered through the window. Stamping them quickly, he handed them back and waved us on with the words, "Don't worry, we know it's all been thoroughly searched!"

After driving in silence for several miles, I stopped the car.

"Let's see what they returned to us," I suggested. "I can't get those films off my mind."

Looking over the things we had been allowed to carry out of the customs office under the watchful eyes of the officials and reporters, we made a startling discovery. All of Bent's metal film containers had been emptied of the exposed film, but three out of the four rolls of film I had taken—including the shots of the closed churches I had vowed would be published in the West—were still in the containers, returned to me in error! I had to look at them several times and have Bent verify what I was seeing before I could believe it.

From the viewpoint of the Russians, if they ever discovered it, this was a lamentable human error. From my viewpoint it was a miracle granted by God's grace. In fact I knew it was both, which only increased my awe to realize again how God could fit anything and everything into His plans. I had long ago given up trying to understand how this was possible.

The day after returning to Copenhagen, I called the

Danish equivalent of the Associated Press, our national news service.

"A friend and I have just been released from arrest at the Russian-Polish border," I announced. "We were questioned for three days by the Russian police."

"Why?"

"We brought Bibles into Russia. I think we have a story you'd want to hear. We'd like to have a news conference tomorrow."

"Why tomorrow?" asked the voice on the other end of the line in an excited tone. "Why not today?"

"Well, I didn't think that was possible."

"How about three hours from now? What's your address?"

Ninna couldn't believe her eyes. She looked on with disbelief as our apartment filled with journalists from many papers and photographers and representatives from radio. Bent and I answered their questions for about an hour, flashbulbs popped, then they all left as quickly as they had come.

The apartment seemed strangely quiet. Bent and Ninna and I sat looking at one another, at a loss for words, our thoughts trying to catch up with everything that had happened—and wondering how the newspapers would report it.

Suddenly we all started to laugh as we realized what the publicity would mean. My threat to the Russian police would be fulfilled beyond anything I had imagined. Once again the persecution of Christians in Russia, the discrimination against them by the Soviet government, and the need for Bibles would be declared by the international secular press.

The next day the story was in newspapers around the world. It made the front page of many Danish papers under such headings as: GAVE OUT BIBLES AND WERE ARRESTED; PASTOR ARRESTED IN THE SOVIET UNION AS BIBLE SMUGGLER; TWO DANES ARRESTED FOR BIBLE

SMUGGLING IN THE SOVIET UNION. There were lengthy articles explaining that we had not broken any laws, but had taken at face value the Soviet government's claims about religious freedom.

The official newspaper of the Danish Communist Party gave its own version under the sarcastic heading, APOSTOLIC SMUGGLER. Accompanied by a picture of Bent and me in our car pointing to where the Bibles had been hidden, the article told of the "modern" hotel in Brest. In order to justify the seriousness with which the Russian authorities had regarded the threat of two unknown Danish citizens whose only weapon was Christian literature, I was described as a modern Paul who set out to conquer the Soviet Union with the Bible, and of course failed due to the enlightenment that science had brought about since the original Paul's more successful assault against the Roman Empire. Typical of the satire was a sentence under the photo: "The Christian church is now saved for the next twenty years in the Soviet Union."

No publicity expert could have designed a better means of promoting the work and objectives of our mission than our arrest at the Russian border. Suddenly everyone in Denmark knew who we were and what we were trying to do. Money began to come in to send Bibles to the East in larger amounts than we had ever dreamed possible. Our arrest, in fact, marked the turning point in the history of our mission.

God had turned what had at first appeared to us as a frightening disaster into a blessing.

5

Detente, Lawbreakers, and Love

When we were no longer able to mail Bibles into Romania, the work of our mission began to flounder and almost came to an end. In those early years the mission was part of the church I pastored, and functioned directly under the board of elders. Many of them did not understand my growing concern for Eastern Europe and were unhappy about the time and attention I was devoting to this work, even though it was done at night after I finished my pastoral duties.

Those were the first days of the thaw in the cold war, when the Western world was beginning to warm to the idea of peaceful coexistence and the French word *detente* was first appearing in newspapers as the expression of this new hope.

Many Christians were tempted to believe that a state of detente could also be reached between Christianity and atheism. This opinion became acceptable among my board of elders, leading some of them to sincerely feel that we should do nothing that would offend the Romanian government, particularly since Romania was seeking to strengthen its trade relationships with Denmark. Some

of the church board felt the mission had accomplished
its original goal by getting many Bibles into Romania and
now should be dissolved.

Articles were appearing in Christian periodicals in the
West saying that conditions in Eastern Europe were not
as bad as some had reported, or were at least getting much
better, and it was argued that interference by outsiders
attempting to help the believers behind the Iron Curtain
only made matters worse.

Oddly enough, it was the secular press that first began
to document the persecution of Christians in the East,
particularly in Russia. Apparently in an attempt to warn
its citizens of what the Kremlin must have considered to
be a national problem of primary concern, the official
Soviet press began to publish articles dealing with the
arrests, trials, and sentencing of believers for such offenses
as sharing one's faith outside of a church, teaching the
Bible to children, and unauthorized gatherings for worship. The story of one eighteen-year-old Russian girl's
arrest reported in Danish papers made a deep impression
upon me at this time.

Maria Braun's crime was teaching children about God.
She and a girlfriend had been conducting Sunday Bible
classes for about eighty children in their village. They
were arrested, the class disbanded, and Maria and Jelena
were sentenced to five years in a labor camp. The judge
agreed with the prosecutor that it was a flagrant violation of the law to teach children about God.

I began to pray daily for these two young women who
had been willing to suffer the consequences of breaking
man's laws in order to obey the laws of God.

The Soviet press was openly denouncing many other
believers as lawbreakers, and newspapers in the West
began to carry the stories of people like Aida Skripnikova.
For distributing on the streets of Leningrad a poem she
had composed that ended with the line, ''Seek God while
He is to be found,'' Aida was arrested and lost her job

and the right to live in Leningrad. This young woman courageously continued to proclaim her faith in spite of prison sentences and psychiatric "treatments." Attacked by numerous articles in the Soviet press, she wrote powerful replies that of course the government press refused to print—antireligious propaganda is allowed but not religious propaganda—but public curiosity about this girl was aroused. People wanted to know what she had done and what she had written, and handwritten copies of her replies to these articles were circulated throughout Russia. Along with the more famous dissidents Solzhenitsyn and Zhakarov, Christian leaders such as Vins, Skripnikova, Prokofiev, and Krutchkov were being vilified in the Soviet press.

I was particularly impressed by the fact that Aida appealed to Christians in the West for help and the fact that believers in Russia had developed an almost incredible secret organization extending across that vast country for the express purpose of documenting the details of persecution and imprisonment and carrying these facts to the West in hope of arousing world opinion to come to their aid. Christians in Russia were also sending appeals for help directly to the United Nations and other world organizations, some in the form of petitions with page after page of signatures attached.

In the face of such overwhelming evidence of the desperate plight of Christians in the East, I was convinced that our mission must increase its efforts and that we must have personal contact with believers in Eastern Europe. Since my own board of elders was not in sympathy with such goals, we agreed to transfer the mission to a larger church in Copenhagen. Eventually I transferred there also, becoming an assistant pastor.

In 1966, a former Bulgarian pastor visited Denmark in an attempt to arouse Christians to pray for and help his persecuted brethren. Arraigned in a show trial after being broken by brainwashing and torture, he and more than a dozen fellow pastors had confessed to crimes they had never committed and were sentenced to lengthy prison terms. After years of appeals, he had at last been allowed to join his family already in the West.

I had the privilege of interpreting for him, from English to Danish, as he traveled through Denmark speaking in many churches. This unusual man, so frail and thin, who spoke with such burning passion, was responsible to a large extent for my first trip into Eastern Europe.

When we first met I told him about the Bibles we had been mailing to Romania. Since it was no longer possible to send them there. I suggested that perhaps we could begin sending them to his country if he would furnish us with addresses.

"Oh, that sort of thing never was possible in Bulgaria," he told me. "But if your mission has the funds, I could give you the names and addresses of some underground pastors in my country who need financial help very badly."

"What do you mean by underground pastors?" I asked. This was a term I had never heard.

Patiently he began to explain. "In my country no church can legally exist without a license from the government, allowing the congregation to meet perhaps once on Sunday and one evening during the week."

"That's not too bad," I replied. "Very few Christians in Denmark attend church any more than that."

"You don't understand!" he exclaimed, becoming excited. "This is the only time you're allowed to be a Christian! You can't worship God at any other time or place; you can't witness, get together for Bible study or even to sing hymns. You're not even supposed to teach your own children about God at home, and according to the law, no one can attend church until he's eighteen!"

I was speechless, stunned by what he was saying. Somehow, the newspaper articles I had read, as bad as they made it sound, hadn't explained this.

"But they're not content with restricting Christianity," he continued. "They close down most of the churches—Protestant, Orthodox, Catholic—and the shrines of other religions. Do you know what *that* means?"

I shook my head. It was impossible for me to comprehend.

"Well, just imagine a congregation of perhaps three hundred believers—and suddenly their license is taken away. It may be for some technicality, but probably no reason is given. The church may be converted into a factory or warehouse, or perhaps it's just torn down to get rid of it."

"Where are these people going to meet?" I asked anxiously.

"Yes, that's the question. Do you think they should stop being Christians now because the government took their license away? The Bible says we're not to forsake the assembling of ourselves together. So they go on meeting in Christ's name, only now it has to be in secret, because they have no legal place to gather. Since they're breaking the law anyway, they decide to meet more often than before, and maybe this starts a revival.

"The Orthodox church is very dead. The small congregations just stand and listen to the priest chant the prayers. Then the Communists close the church, and the people cry out to God in their homes. That's when something new happens. They come to know Christ in a personal way and God begins to talk to them and guide them. Small groups of believers spring up everywhere.

"Most of them have no Bibles. Who's going to teach them? This is what these underground pastors do. The secret congregations they serve are very poor because it's difficult for a Christian to obtain decent employment, and they're forced to pay heavy fines whenever they're caught in illegal meetings. Many of them are in and out of prison all their lives. These pastors travel unnoticed from town to town, visiting small groups of Christians who are meeting in secret—in their homes, in the woods—and they teach them from the Scriptures."

A fire had begun to burn within me as he spoke. "I'm sure our mission would like to support men like that!" I said, determined that by God's grace these suffering members of Christ's body would not be forgotten by the church in the West.

"I will tell you how to contact some of them!" The lines in his face had suddenly changed directions as he broke into a broad smile. "And I'll also give you the names of people in Bulgaria who can receive Bibles for distribution. You'll need couriers willing to trust God to get them across the border with the Bibles."

The new mission board began to pray about this idea. We decided definitely that we would like to help support needy pastors in the East, and we began to pray for couriers to take the Bibles and the funds. The first step, logically, would be for me to make an extensive visit myself in order to lay the foundation.

Shortly after I became an assistant pastor of the church in Copenhagen, the board of elders there agreed to give me a month's leave of absence for my first trip behind the Iron Curtain. I was able to receive an official invitation to Romania as a visiting pastor, giving me the right to preach in registered churches—a policy that was soon after discontinued.

A close friend from Copenhagen, Rene Hartzner, decided to take a month off from his business to accompany me. We were advised to take very few Bibles, since this was our first trip. We each brought only about ten.

Rene and I were unprepared for what we saw: churches with all the seats removed so that the congregation could stand, packed tightly together from wall to wall; singing that seemed unearthly in its beauty and urgency and left us choked with emotion; faces literally aglow with a heavenly love and joy; meetings that went on for four or five hours because these believers wanted to take full advantage of the small liberty they had.

And the tears! So many tears in so many eyes. Always. We tried to describe them to one another as tears of joy, and so they seemed, but they had another quality, something deep and solemn, that made us suspect that the joy these people knew was somehow of a nature very different from ours.

What an experience to give one of these believers a Bible! To see the look of amazement and then joy. To be hugged, kissed on both cheeks, then hugged again. To see them fondle that Bible, turn its pages reverently, kiss it repeatedly, and then tell us that they had just received the answer to many years of prayer. They would ask us if Christians in Denmark were free to meet for worship anywhere they wished; if we could have "extra" meetings at church or even in homes; if we could talk to people about Christ on the street; if we could really teach children from the Bible; if there were really enough Bibles to go around, and enough song books too; if we were allowed to print gospel literature and hand it out on the streets and even invite people to come to our churches?

They savored each nod of our heads in response to these questions as though it were a delicious morsel. My heart was smitten as I thought of the empty churches in Denmark and Bibles lying neglected in nearly every home. Rene and I discussed with one another whether persecution was, after all, the most healthy climate for Christianity and something we needed in Denmark to divide the sheep from the goats. Could it be that the only way to discover whether we really believed would be to see if we were willing to suffer the loss of a job, or imprisonment, or even death for the faith we professed so glibly?

We noticed that the Christians, with few exceptions, seemed to represent the poorest class in a supposedly classless society, yet they didn't complain about persecution and discrimination. Nor did the Christians in Communist countries consider themselves anti-Communists. They were willing to "render unto Caesar the things that are Caesar's," but when the state denied them the right to "render unto God the things that are God's," they felt bound by their consciences to remain true to their Lord.

Instead of the bitterness we had expected to find, we experienced a Christlike love that exposed the shallowness of our own lives—a love so open, so warm, so simple and asking nothing in return while showering its affection upon us that Rene and I literally seemed impotent to respond. One incident in particular near the end of our stay in Romania caused us both to cry out to God to give us this same capacity of selfless concern for others that these Christians were expressing to us.

We had attended a registered church in a village. The small, frame building was built to seat perhaps 150, but there must have been 600 people packed inside, with more peering through the windows. The service lasted nearly five hours.

This was a Pentecostal church in an area where there had been about 10,000 Pentecostals in 1954. Now there were more than 100,000! The pastor told us that quite a number of the people there that day were secret believers who didn't yet have the courage to confess their faith openly for fear of losing their jobs. This was something he never tried to push on anyone, leaving that persuasion entirely to the Holy Spirit.

As we walked back to our hotel in a city adjacent to the village, about a dozen of the believers accompanied us, crowding around like affectionate children. The quality of love they expressed to us during that walk of about three miles, the comradeship we enjoyed together, the sense of oneness as members of the body of Christ, engulfed us in an almost ecstatic euphoria that left us feeling weak, floundering dizzily in a love that embarrassed and confused us.

Arriving at our hotel, Rene and I said an abrupt good-night—and good-bye. We were both exhausted after such a long meeting and the prolonged intercourse with people whose spiritual strength was so much greater than our own. We had to leave early in the morning and needed to sleep. Entering the hotel, we left these brothers and sisters in Christ, who had accompanied us such a long way, standing with wistful expressions on the sidewalk outside.

From the window of our tenth-floor room, I followed their slow, almost reluctant progress back toward the village, until they disappeared over a wooded hill in the distance.

"My heart is breaking right now because of the way we just treated them," I said to Rene.

Sitting on the edge of his bed, he was looking down at the floor and shaking his head. "I can't believe it," he said almost inaudibly, "that we would just wash our hands of them like that! What hellish selfishness made us respond to their love that way? I know they wanted to be invited in—I knew it then—but I wanted to get rid of them so I could get some sleep. I wouldn't even take time for a cup of coffee after they had come all that way. What are they thinking now?"

The sleep I had thought so important eluded me for a long time that night. Rene's words kept repeating themselves over and over in my mind: "I wanted to get rid of them, I wanted to get rid of them, I wanted to get rid of them!" This was my confession, too. I never would have believed myself capable of such selfish callousness—and toward people who had showed us such love!

I had founded a mission to help such believers, had urged the church in Denmark to get involved, and had prided myself that I was willing to go behind the Iron Curtain to do something for the cause, which was more than most people would do. But in that very process of doing what I had thought was so much, the shallowness of my own love had been exposed.

There was a limit, after all, in how far I was willing to go. And that night I had been startled to discover how close that limit was to nothing at all.

6

What Christianity Is This?

Although it was only eight in the evening, the dimly lit streets of Sofia were already semideserted. This was the end of October and the nip of fall was in the air, accented by a biting wind that swirled out of alleys and down the broad avenues in gusts that stung cheeks and eyes and chased leaves and papers along the usually impeccably clean sidewalks. There were a few hardy evening strollers making slow progress as they paused to inspect the sparse displays of merchandise in shop windows, but most of the intermittent pedestrian traffic, collars buttoned, clutching hats and skirts at each new gust of wind, hurried homeward.

Rene and I stood shivering on the sidewalk under a pale, yellow light, trying to read the name of the street and correlate it with the map we carried. The street names were printed in the Greek and Latin characters common to Slavic languages, whereas our map listed only the Latin equivalents. It was a difficult enough problem in daylight for someone speaking Bulgarian, but hopeless for us in the dark. We were carrying substantial funds for two underground pastors and had intended to locate their homes that afternoon, but our plane had been inexplicably delayed, making the difference between afternoon and evening, light and dark, forcing us to abandon any hope of finding either pastor's house that night— and we had to leave for a similar mission in another city early the next morning.

Our one remaining hope was to locate a registered Protestant church in Sofia that had a meeting that very night. Perhaps one of the pastors would be present. A tiny dot on our map marked the location of the church, but how to find our way to it? That was the insurmountable problem occupying us now.

Rene was glancing back and forth from the map to a street name posted high on a building, trying to locate our present position in relation to that tiny dot. I had given up trying to help him, and was praying, which seemed to me the most effective thing I could do. If that failed, I was prepared to abandon the project entirely and get back to our hotel. Already we were attracting too much attention.

I was worried. We had tried to ask directions from several passersby who seemed the least likely to be agents of the secret police, but the only response had been a stiffened back and a quickened pace. Conversations with Westerners must be reported to the authorities, and no one willingly put himself in that position without good reason.

"We're never going to locate that church ourselves," said Rene at last, folding the map and stuffing it back into his pocket with a sigh of resignation. "I know the main street we're on now, but I can't make out the cross streets. I don't even know what direction is north or south. Look, why don't we stop this nonsense and get a cab!"

"I'm as new at this as you are," I replied helplessly. "We have a lot of money with us, and a lot of people to see before we leave Bulgaria, and . . . well, I don't want to announce our arrival to the . . ."

"If this place is as full of informers as we've been told," said Rene skeptically, "the local gendarmes have probably received a dozen reports of two idiots with a map lost in the middle of Sofia. That's not going to cause a red alert, as inept as we must look." He shoved his hands into his pockets and stamped his feet. "I'm freezing."

"May I help you?" asked a soft, feminine voice in German.

We turned to see a girl of about twenty, bundled up in a long coat, a kerchief on her head, standing a few feet away and peering inquisitively at us in the dim light.

The elusive feeling of uneasiness that had been gnawing at me suddenly grew stronger.

"We're looking for Gorky Street," I said, trying to sound relaxed and nonchalant.

"What number on Gorky Street?"

"Oh, no number in particular," I responded quickly, brushing her impertinent curiosity aside. "Just Gorky Street—anywhere on it. Tell us how to get there, and we can find our way after that."

"But you must be seeking a particular address," she insisted. "What number is it? Perhaps we're going in the same direction." A half-amused smile was beginning to form on her face.

That she should walk up to two strange men, obviously Westerners, and engage them in conversation was more than enough to arouse my suspicions. But to insistently inquire about our exact destination—now I was sure she must be from the secret police. Yet she appeared so innocent, this wisp of a girl, staring wide-eyed, looking from one to the other of us as though she had seen us somewhere before.

I glanced at Rene, but a shadow hid the expression on his face.

"After all, it's a registered church," I thought to myself. "It would be even more suspicious now if I don't tell her."

And then aloud: "We would like to go to number thirty-seven."

"Praise God!" she exclaimed. "I was praying at home and the Lord told me to come and lead two men from the West to our church. This isn't the way I go."

Glancing apprehensively up and down the street, she added quickly in a low voice: "Follow me about twenty paces back and I'll lead you there."

Rene and I looked at one another and went limp. We set off down the street together, following this Bulgarian girl as though she were an angel from heaven.

The church was indistinguishable from other buildings in its neighborhood. When we entered the front door she was waiting for us in a small foyer. The service had already begun.

"Go up to the balcony," she whispered, pointing to a rough, wooden stairway. "I'll see you afterward." She stepped through a door into the sanctuary as we turned to climb the stairs.

The church was crowded. We stood at the back of the balcony, hesitating, looking for a seat. Several people turned around and noticed us. A short, dark man sitting on the aisle motioned toward the front row where people were already whispering and squeezing closer together to make room.

The balcony ran the entire length of one side of the building. Our place in the front row gave us a good view of the platform and of most of the congregation below. The singing had an indescribable spiritual quality that lifted and captured and made one feel a part of something truly beyond this world. I felt myself caught up in a rising crescendo of glory, and tears rolled down my cheeks as I realized the immediate oneness I felt with these members of Christ's body who seemed to me, from their lives and the persecution I knew they suffered, so much like the early church. It strengthened my confidence in the Scriptures just to be there and to see for myself that same triumphant faith of Bible days still alive and conquering on this earth. Looking around the room at upturned, shining faces, to my joy I suddenly recognized a man on the far side of the church. I knew him from his photograph. One of the pastors we had come to see!

This was the prayer meeting. Everyone knelt on the hard wood floor. I couldn't understand a word they were saying, but I knew they were talking to God. I felt His presence in the room. I had warned people how deceptive and unreliable feelings can be—but still I *felt* God was there. I *felt* that they were talking to Him and He was listening, and I *knew* that I was touching reality, feeling within my spirit a dimension entirely beyond my five senses.

That wasn't all I felt. As the fervent prayers followed one after another, on and on, I felt the rough planks cutting into my knees. That sensation soon became so overwhelming that the spiritual reality receded from my consciousness. I became aware of only one thing, that I inhabited a body of flesh and bone, and my knees were crying out for relief from the pain inflicted upon them by the hard ridges in the worn plank flooring. Sensing a movement by my side, I opened my eyes momentarily to see Rene get up stiffly and painfully to resume his seat on the bench. No one else had found that necessary, neither the old women nor small children. Prayers were still pouring forth with unabated fervor, faces and hands upraised. These people were not behind an Iron Curtain as we had thought—they were in heaven.

But I was on earth. Only my pride and fear of the shame I would feel kept me from joining Rene. I managed, through sheer willpower, to hang on until the end of the last prayer.

The congregation stood for the closing hymn and the church service had ended. Before I could turn to leave, I felt a hand upon my shoulder. Startled, I looked around to discover who it could be, and found myself face-to-face with the other pastor we had come to see!

"Praise God, Brother Kristian!" he exclaimed in English, embracing me warmly. "We've been expecting you!"

I was stunned. He had never seen me before, couldn't possibly know my name—even my wife hadn't known where Rene and I were going. Our plans had been kept a complete secret, known only to ourselves and God.

Partially recovering from the shock, I replied in a low voice, "I'll see you at your home later tonight." Then I turned away, knowing that the official pastor of this church, whom we had been warned was collaborating with the Communists, would be required to report the names of members of his congregation seen conversing at any length with visitors from the West.

People were greeting us with tears of joy, kissing us on both cheeks, hugging us, pumping our arms up and down with hearty handshakes, making us forget our bruised knees and feel once again that ecstatic love and unity in Christ so real to them.

Making our way slowly downstairs, Rene and I momentarily found ourselves in the crowded hallway next to Sonya, the girl who had met us on the street.

"Tell Pastor Korbut to go home and we'll see him later," I said quickly, naming the other pastor whose face I had recognized among the congregation during the meeting. "And please! We need you to guide us! Can you meet us in about thirty minutes at the Lenin Monument?"

She nodded and moved on through the crowd.

The pastor had seen us now. Pushing his way through the departing congregation, he greeted us each with a firm handclasp and welcomed us warmly in German. He told us how happy he was that we were there, what a good thing it was for tourists from the West to be able to see for themselves the freedom of religion in his country, that he hoped we would tell the truth about this when we got home and also bring fraternal greetings from the Christians in Bulgaria to those in Denmark.

I felt sorry for him. He was trying so hard. For another ten minutes he told us of the beauties of the Black Sea, the beaches, the hotels, the restaurants, the warmth and healthful qualities of the sun and water, and urged us by all means to include at least one seaside resort in our trip. It would be a pity—unforgivable—not to visit the Black Sea. To miss that would be to miss the real flavor and spirit of Bulgaria. With such mundane pleasantries, all delivered in a stiffly formal and labored attempt to seem friendly, he managed to keep us under his eyes and occupied until all of the congregation had left.

Sonya was waiting for us, pretending to be engrossed in window-shopping, when we arrived five minutes late for our rendezvous. She noticed us when we were still a block away, and began to walk down the street. We followed, keeping at a safe distance. After we had walked in this manner for about a mile, she slowed down until we caught up with her.

"This is it," said Sonya softly, pausing at last in front of a small, square frame structure with a wide, covered porch. A faint glow around one window indicated that someone was still awake in the house. She pushed carefully on a gate, whispering, "It squeaks!"

We stepped into the front yard. Instead of going up onto the porch, however, she turned onto a narrow stone walk that led to the rear. I assumed that we were entering by a back door, but she continued past the house. After a few yards I saw against the sky the outline of another house behind the first one. Following the narrow walkway, we continued past that one also until we came to a third, smaller than the other two.

"Doesn't Pastor Korbut live in the front house?" I asked softly, worried that she might be taking us to the wrong place.

"He used to," she whispered, "but a few months ago the secret police moved into his house and put him back here.

"I'm sure God kept you from finding this street and sent me to guide you, not just to church but here, also. If you had come yourselves, you would have knocked at the front house and asked the secret police for Pastor Korbut!" She clutched her head with both hands. "That would have gone very hard for him! He's just been re- leased from prison. They tortured him—and he broke."

Indeed, Pastor Korbut looked like a broken man. There was a smile on his face when he ushered us excitedly into his humble dwelling, but it was weak and strained, trembling on the surface. He seemed worn and thin, older than his years. A tall, stooping man, he moved about the room dragging two extra chairs from a corner, not just with a limp, but as though every step brought pain, which brought a memory that increased the pain. Having seated us with all the dignity and hospitality of a prince, he sank back into a chair with a sigh.

Something vital was missing in his eyes. They lacked depth, as though his soul had been torn from his body.

The Korbut family spoke only Bulgarian, so Sonya inter- preted everything into German for us, adding bits on the side about this pastor's recent arrest, until we knew the whole pathetic story.

Some months before, a visitor from Sweden had been given a letter to take out of the country, to be mailed in Greece in order to avoid the Bulgarian censors. While in Greece, however, he had forgotten to mail the letter. It was discovered in his briefcase during the course of a thorough search by the border guards when he passed through Bulgaria again on his way back to Western Europe. The unsigned letter was addressed to the Bulgar- ian pastor now living in the West that I had interpreted for when he had visited Denmark. Pastor Korbut was arrested and tortured in an effort to make him divulge who had written the letter, although it contained nothing more than Christian greetings.

For years Pastor Korbut had had a circulatory weakness

in his legs. Knowing this, the police forced him to stand hour after hour during intensive questioning, until his legs swelled so badly that he could no longer endure the pain. Eventually he had collapsed. In this condition, unable to bear the tortures any longer, he had gasped out the name of the person who had written the letter—another underground pastor. He had been released and the other pastor arrested.

Since that day, unable to forgive himself for betraying a fellow believer, Pastor Korbut had been tormented by an unremitting sense of shame and remorse so overwhelming that it seemed even more unbearable than the physical torture that had broken him in prison.

"Some of Christ's commands are impossible for us to obey under present conditions," said Pastor Korbut. "For instance, the command to 'go into all the world preaching the gospel.' We cannot go to other countries." He shrugged and that weak smile brightened momentarily. "So we must do our best here in our own country. It is difficult." His eyes closed and his face clouded with a look of pain and sorrow. "You cannot know how difficult it is."

Mrs. Korbut reached over and put a tiny, worn hand on one of her husband's.

His expression brightened again and he leaned forward in his chair. "We can pray for those who go into all the world. Someone must pray. This we have learned to do. But we need news from other countries in order to know what to pray for, so I hope you will pardon us for asking so many questions."

He seemed overwhelmed by our visit, to think that we cared enough to travel many miles to see him, that the church in Bulgaria, suffering so much, was at least not forgotten in the West; that we were actually praying for him and for the secret congregations he pastored.

Tears rolled down his cheeks when we handed him the money we had brought. A glance around their tiny apartment was enough to assure us that the Korbuts needed it badly. But both he and his wife protested strongly that it was too much. Before finally accepting it, Mrs. Korbut put an arm around her husband and, faces turned upward, weeping, oblivious to our presence for that brief moment, they thanked God together.

It was getting late. We stood to leave. The Korbuts embraced us fervently. They both seemed brighter, as though a burden had been lifted.

Following Sonya back out into the street in the darkness, I had a strong feeling that we had brought more than money. As badly as that was needed, they had a greater need—the reassurance that Christ understood and forgave, that they were not abandoned by their heavenly Father. I was sure that this was the main gift that He had sent us to bring them, and my heart was glad.

Reaching the street, Sonya continued on the way by which we had come. At the next corner, however, she turned left for one block, then left again. We were now retracing our steps, but on the next street over, paralleling the one we had taken earlier in the evening. My curiosity about this intriguing maneuver could not be contained.

"Why did you do that?" I asked.

"But you never go back the same way," she whispered. "There are informers in every block."

"Awake this late at night?" asked Rene incredulously.

"One never knows. Is it worth the chance to save a few steps?"

Neither of us replied. She seemed to sense what we felt.

"There's no way I can explain to a Westerner what this system has done to our country. We never know who the informers are. It could be someone in one's own family. This breaks down the natural affection and trust that there ought to be between human beings. You're suspicious of everyone—sometimes even of other believers. It's terrible!"

"I don't think I could live here," said Rene.

"We have no other alternative. If we did..."

The unfinished sentence was still hanging in the air when we arrived at Pastor Tisjkob's house fifteen minutes later, where the door opened promptly to our quiet knock.

"All day we've been expecting you!" he exclaimed, giving me a hug. "We've been longing to see you!"

"This I don't understand!" I said, feeling confused. "Nobody knows our traveling route. Even my wife doesn't know I'm here today, so how could you know I was coming?"

"God in heaven knows," he responded simply, and pointed upward. His face was shining with an expression of childish innocence.

"And my name! How did you know that?" I insisted. The question had been burning in my mind ever since he had whispered my name in the church. Surely none of our couriers would have told him! They knew better than to let information slip that could become a noose around this pastor's neck during interrogation.

Pastor Tisjkob shrugged and gave me the same enigmatic reply. "God in heaven knows." The expression on his face told me that for him this was explanation enough. It was so simple: what God in heaven knows, He tells to His children on earth when they need to know.

"Yes, I realize that God in heaven knows everything," I responded with a helpless laugh. "But how did you know?"

He shrugged. "See my daughter over there?" He pointed to a thin, intelligent-looking girl who had been staring at me with a strange fascination ever since I had come into the room.

I nodded.

"She's just nine years old. About a week ago she had a dream. In it she saw two men wearing western clothes, sitting in the balcony of our church. One of them had lots of dark hair like your friend. The other one was quite bald, just like you." He laughed good-naturedly and then continued. "But what impressed her the most was a white handkerchief sticking out of the bald man's suit pocket."

Looking down at my pocket, I saw the white hand-kerchief. I had intended to change from this obviously western suit to a darker, older one that would be less noticeable on the streets of Sofia, but because our plane was late, I hadn't done it.

"She had never seen anyone wearing a handkerchief like that in her life," continued Pastor Tisjkob. "She talked about it all week."

Rene and I were exchanging glances. This was almost too much.

"But my name," I persisted, struggling to comprehend what he was saying.

"We understood that this dream had special significance, so we prayed for the Lord to give us the interpretation. Last night my wife had the same dream. In it the Lord told her that your name was Kristian, and that you were coming to see us."

I leaned back in my chair and looked over at Rene again. He seemed as nonplussed as I was. We both believed that God uses miracles and visions today, but I could see that he was having the same problem I was accepting a story like this.

It wasn't that I doubted Pastor Tisjkob. I was sure he was telling the truth. But I was staggered by the relationship these people had with God, because it raised a devastating question: If this was Christianity, then what was the game we were playing in the West?

7

War and Peace

"Look! Look! Up high—over there!"

I gave the ball a hard kick and turned to see what my friend was shouting about. Other children on the school playground were pointing into the sky, too, as the deafening roar of engines swept over us like a flowing river of sound.

Then I saw them, high overhead, airplanes in formation, wave after wave of them, diving down upon the center of Copenhagen.

Our soccer game forgotten, we stood motionless in stunned fascination. Somewhere someone shouted, "Hurrah! Hurrah! The English are here to rescue us! Hurrah! Hurrah!"

Immediately the whole school, outside for recess, took up the chant: "Hurrah! Hurrah! The English are here to rescue us! Hurrah! Hurrah!"

We children were too young—I was just twelve—to understand that the bombs were aimed at the headquarters of the German occupation forces and other military installations in Copenhagen, or that many of them would miss their target and wreak vengeance upon friend as well as upon foe. From the school yard on a hill overlooking the city we had an unobstructed view on this beautiful cloudless March day of the tons of bombs dropping from the sky like clusters of long fat eggs. As we watched destruction rain upon our city, heard and felt the shock of distant explosions, saw the flames erupt and a pall of heavy, acrid smoke settle below us, we didn't think of familiar buildings crumbling, friends dying. We only knew it meant the beginning of the end for the Germans who had occupied our country, and we danced and cheered the planes and bombs as though our liberators could hear us.

At home my mother was praying fervently. There were four of us children at four different schools—and the radio was saying that a school had been hit by bombs and all the children killed. When we four and my father had all reached home safely, arriving one by one throughout an afternoon that seemed to my mother an eternity, our family gathered together in the living room to thank God for His mercy upon us, and to pray for the others who had not been so fortunate. The bombs had wrecked a French school near the center of the city, killing and wounding hundreds.

The war caused many people in Denmark to think more seriously about their relationship to God, at least temporarily. I witnessed scenes that made me even as a young boy, ponder the meaning of life, and that left memories which would never be forgotten. Fixed in my mind forever were the German soldiers firing into a long line of people waiting to buy bread, the surprised expression on the face of the first man I ever saw hit by bullets, the five-day strike in Copenhagen that cut off all food, water, electricity, the barbed-wire barricade the German troops built that ran close to our house and encircled the city, the young man, curly blond hair flying, trying to flee this barrier with his aged grandmother on a three-wheeled bicycle cart.

Such experiences made me very conscious of how fragile life was and of my need to prepare to meet God.

My mother gathered us children together every evening for prayer. Father joined in, too, as we sang old hymns, read from the Bible, and asked God to take care of us and to restore freedom to our country. My father had lost his business to the Depression in 1932; and again, when he had built another, the Germans took that away when they occupied Denmark. It was troubles like these that kept our family praying together. I grew up with a strong belief that God was alive and real, ready to help if we would call upon Him.

Shortly after the war I was confirmed in the Lutheran state church of Denmark where I had been baptized as an infant. Confirmation is a milestone marking the passage out of childhood into young adulthood. In fact, this is the biggest event in a young person's life, with parties, gifts from relatives and friends—something that no fourteen-year-old would want to miss. That is one reason why about 90 percent of the Danes belong to the state church.

However, very few people attend church regularly—no more than five percent. For the Danes, Christianity is not so much a way of life as a heritage one possesses from birth. One's relationship to God is something taken for granted, a closed subject not even to be discussed—finished and done with by the ceremonies of infant baptism and confirmation. Beyond that, what one does with his religion is his own business.

As a boy I grew up with the implicit understanding that I was a Christian simply because I belonged to the church. I believed in God, and took my religion very seriously. However, I was afraid to let my friends know that I attended church regularly for fear of losing their respect. None of them or their parents ever went into a church—except for confirmation ceremonies, weddings and funerals, or for Christmas or Easter services.

Our family usually attended a large cathedral that seated

about 2,000. On a typical Sunday morning there would be about thirty-five in the congregation. I don't recall that anyone was particularly discouraged about this. It was considered normal, and gave some of us the chance to feel more righteous than others because we were the "faithful few" that the priest could count upon to be in attendance.

The priest who did much of the preaching at the cathedral was a good friend of my parents, and we Kristian children were the same ages as his. Our two families often spent holidays together. I liked him as a person. He was fun to be with, but as I reached my middle teens it bothered me increasingly that he had a policy not to talk about God or religion on his days off. In fact, he didn't talk very much about God in the pulpit. His sermons were mostly politics and philosophy, or psychology and social reform.

One Sunday, when we were too late to get to the cathedral, my mother took us to a state church much closer to our home. A very serious, fervent priest was in the pulpit that morning, preaching a sermon entirely based upon the Bible. This was what I had wanted to hear. It seemed more solid than the human wisdom preached at the cathedral. I returned to listen attentively to this biblical priest as often as I could.

In this church there was a wealthy and rather eccentric man, who seemed to me to have some very strange ideas about religion. He placed himself squarely in front of me after the service one Sunday, fixed me with a piercing glare, and demanded to know whether I was *saved*. This was an unfamiliar expression, but I presumed it had something to do with getting to heaven. That, in my opinion, was something no one could know until he died—but if anyone was going to make it, I certainly was. I told him that I had been baptized and confirmed like anyone else, and let him know by implication that anything beyond that was none of his or anyone else's business. I avoided this peculiar man whenever possible, and took comfort in noting that nearly everyone else in the church seemed to feel the same way toward him as I did.

One day about six months after I had started attending this new church, a close friend and I were sitting in front of my house discussing what we wanted to be when we got out of school. We were both seventeen and had been friends since we were five.

"Well, there's more to life than getting a job and earning money," I said earnestly. "We have to remember that it goes on beyond the grave and must prepare for that as well."

"I've wanted for a long time to know about God, Hans," said Arne. It was an astonishing admission and I countered with my only solution.

"The only way is to go to church," I urged him. He came with me the following Sunday to hear the biblical priest, and began attending regularly.

I soon noticed a remarkable change in Arne. We had always argued a great deal and often our disputes ended in real knockdown fights. But now Arne had changed. I couldn't fight with him anymore. This bothered me a great deal, and I began to suspect that he had gotten something from the sermons that I had been too proud to accept for myself.

"What has happened to you, Arne?" I asked him one day after struggling for a week to get the courage to broach the subject. "You've changed so much!"

"I've been saved, Hans!" he replied enthusiastically. "I didn't know how to tell you, so I'm glad you asked. It's wonderful! Everything's different now!"

"Oh, no!" I thought, "not *that*—the same thing that old eccentric talks about!" I was mad enough to explode, but held my temper with great effort.

Aloud, I said, "I told you to go to church—you know that—and now that you've been going for six months you think you're better than I am. Well, maybe you don't know it, but I've been going to church all my life!"

"But you're a sinner, Hans," said Arne unapologetically.

Now I *was* angry! I could have started a fist fight with him right then, but I wanted help so badly that I held my temper. For weeks I had been struggling inwardly for the courage to go to the church to talk alone with the biblical priest, but Arne was my age and would understand even better. It wasn't easy to ask Arne for help, but I was desperate.

"Arne, I'd like you to tell me about it," I began. "I mean how it happened to you, and..." I hesitated, groping for words.

Jumping suddenly to his feet, Arne looked at his wristwatch and exclaimed, "I almost forgot...I've got an appointment! Some other time, Hans. I'm sorry!" He turned abruptly and ran off down the street.

Now I was fuming. "First he tells me he's saved and I'm a sinner," I thought, "and then when I sincerely ask him to help me, he says he has no time. Some Christian he is! What a Pharisee!"

That night I awakened with Arne's words hammering at my conscience: "You're a sinner, Hans! You're a sinner, Hans!" I had great difficulty getting back to sleep as I fought against what I was too proud to admit. I was very religious and tried to live uprightly. I had been baptized and confirmed. Then what was this talk about being saved, and why did it happen to Arne after he'd only been going to church a few months and I had been going all my life?

For two days and nights this battle went on inside. Tormented by those words, "You're a sinner, Hans!" I had no appetite and couldn't sleep.

The third day I was riding a streetcar, standing up in the back because I felt too miserable to sit next to anyone. A drunk climbed aboard and started unsteadily down the aisle to find a seat when he saw me and lurched over to engage me in conversation. I couldn't stand the smell of his breath, but worse than that, I was very proud of the company I kept and was afraid some friend might see me standing next to him. His eyes were bloodshot, his speech slurred, and his clothes were filthy and torn.

Turning my back, I moved to the other side of the car, but he staggered after me, pouring out the details of his unhappy and frustrated life. Too concerned with my own problems to care about his, I fled from side to side of that tram with him persistently lurching after me, belching up the smell of half-digested alcohol while spitting out a disgusting and confused tale of frustrations and disappointments. He had been spurned by several girls, lost his job times without number because of drinking, tried to escape the habit but couldn't find the moral strength. I was about to give up trying to keep one step ahead of him on the back platform and attempt an escape down the aisle to a seat, when something this obnoxious pest said stopped me.

"I know I'm a sinner," he sobbed bitterly, slobbering down the front of his stained and torn shirt. Those words sounded like a trumpet blast in my ears, I grabbed him by the arm.

"Then you're one of the happiest men in the world!" I exclaimed, shaking him so he would be sure to hear what I said.

"No! I'm the most miserable man in the world," he whimpered.

"But you said you're a sinner! Don't you know that Jesus died on the cross for sinners just like you?"

Peering at me from beneath drooping eyelids, he cocked his head to one side, and a spark of comprehension seemed to ignite in his eyes. "Now that's something my mother used to tell me," he said solemnly. "She's been praying for me for years."

"Well, your mother's right," I continued eagerly, feeling excited for him. The solution to *his* problems was so easy! "Jesus died for sinners, and you're a sinner. Call upon

Him—He'll save you! The Bible says so!"

Tears were rolling down his cheeks. "Oh, I'll do it!" he exclaimed. Hanging onto the back of a seat, swaying drunkenly, he turned his face upward and began praying aloud, asking Jesus to forgive him and to come into his heart.

Before my startled gaze I saw an incredible transformation take place. Suddenly the expression on his face had changed from one of drunken stupidity to alert intelligence. Peace and joy were radiating from his eyes, and he seemed the most beautiful person I had ever met.

In that moment, with a sudden insight that took me by surprise, I saw something else—that man's relationship to God depends upon grace alone, not on the good deeds I had prided myself in and which had prevented me so long from being able to admit that I was a sinner. Like a revelation from heaven, I saw the pride, rebellion, and selfish willfulness of my own heart. I was as great a sinner as the world had ever seen. Suddenly I was glad that Jesus had died for *me*. Surrendering the pride that had barred the door whenever Christ had knocked before, I opened my heart—and in that very moment I knew He came in to stay.

"I'm saved, too!" I exclaimed, shaking his hand. We stood there beaming at each other like two children who had stumbled upon a treasure. Then we both burst into a laugh, a new kind of laugh that I had never experienced before. It felt as though a fountain of joy had begun to bubble and dance within me.

As we left the tram and walked down the street together, something inside of me was singing over and over the chorus of an old hymn: "This is my story, to God be the glory, I'm only a sinner saved by grace." These words had often angered or embarrassed me. I had sat in petulant silence as others sang them, but now this chorus had become *my* song, and I was bursting with the joy of knowing that God had forgiven *me* because of

Christ. I felt clean, and light, and free.

Brothers now, little children in God's family, we talked excitedly as we walked, until we came to a corner where he had to turn to the right and I to the left. Standing there on the sidewalk, saying good-bye, but loath to part, I was vaguely aware that we were in front of the house of the priest whose sermons had started me thinking about how one really becomes a Christian. Suddenly we embraced fervently. It was a spontaneous act, so unlike me, and took me by surprise. I felt such love in my heart for this man, and such happiness that we had helped one another to enter the kingdom of God together.

We parted with a long, tight embrace that awakened a new, almost ecstatic sense of brotherhood within me, not just for him, but for all the other members of this forever family.

Relaxing our grip upon each other at last, we said good-bye again, and each turned to go his own way. Then I saw the priest's son, who was just my age, looking out the window, a startled expression on his face. He knew me as a proud hypocrite, and he had watched in amazement as I had embraced this filthy tramp.

Surprised at my own lack of embarrassment, I waved to him and set off happily down the street toward home, humming my new song.

8

Refugees and Revival

From that day I was a different person. My religion had turned into a relationship, not just with a church, but now with the living God. Worship—once something to stage with props and promptings—ceased to be a matter of form and ritual, and became instead a spontaneous part of life, possible anywhere and at any time. I found myself talking with God as though He were really there and listening. Often our conversation became so intimate that I forgot that I was praying—a practice that had once been a difficult and burdensome duty.

This new and wonderfully real sense of a *personal* relationship to God through the resurrected Christ living in *me* brought a growing realization that God must have a plan for my life. This, however, I imagined as something in the future rather than the present. I knew nothing as yet of the day-by-day guidance that God gives to those who expect this from Him.

In 1954, having completed business college and my military service, I went to Hamburg, Germany, where I spent a year in apprenticeship, at no salary, for a large wholesale-retail building-supply distributor. My training covered every aspect of the business—buying, selling, setting prices, checking profits—that I would need to operate the Danish wholesale business, which I was expected to take over one day from my father.

There was no Berlin Wall as yet, and East Germans by the tens of thousands were turning their backs on the Communist "paradise" to flee into West Berlin. From Berlin, Hamburg alone was receiving more than a thousand refugees a day in its processing camps where they were temporarily housed until they could be absorbed into other parts of the country. One of these camps, which normally contained about ten thousand refugees, was located on an old military base that had inexplicably escaped the Allied bombs. Living conditions were horrible, with as many as twenty people crowded into each of the tiny rooms partitioned off in the old barracks. These were people who had escaped with little more than the clothes on their backs, people to whom freedom was worth the loss of the accumulated savings and possessions of a lifetime.

I joined an independent youth group involved in spreading the gospel at this large refugee camp. We would walk through the barracks singing hymns, passing out tracts, and inviting everyone to our meetings. Each week we gathered about five hundred children together in an old garage for Sunday school, and following that we usually had about three hundred adults in another meeting. As a result, many among both children and adults received Christ.

At this camp I had my first contact with people from Eastern Europe, never dreaming that one day my life would be devoted to spreading the gospel in that area of the world. Some of these escapees were Christians, and I remember, in my zeal, reproving them for leaving their country.

"But they need your Christian witness back *there!*" I argued one Sunday afternoon as I scolded a young escapee who had just arrived at the camp. "If all the Christians escape, who's going to tell the people that are left about Christ?"

"How can you be my judge, when you don't know what it's like to live in East Germany?" replied the handsome young man quietly. There was pain and sorrow in his voice, as though I had uncovered a deep wound. "I was the best student in my class, yet they told me I wasn't intelligent enough to continue, and made me quit school when I was fifteen—because I was a Christian. For years the teachers had tried to get me to abandon my faith, but I could not deny Christ. I would rather die.

"I tried to get a job as an apprentice to learn a trade. I was willing to do anything. But people in my town were afraid to hire me. They knew I'd been put out of school for being a Christian. I didn't want to leave my parents, or my town, or the friends in my church. But after three years of picking up odd jobs here and there, with no opportunity to use the intelligence and the talents God had given me, I knew there was no other way. On my eighteenth birthday, I said to my parents, 'Mother and Father, I thank you for everything you've done for me, especially that you brought me up to believe in Jesus Christ as my Savior. I love you very much, and I don't want to leave you, but I have no future here.'

"We embraced one another and cried. The look on my mother's face nearly killed me—but they didn't tell me not to go. I don't know if I'll ever see them again on this earth."

There was a Christian family with whom I had become acquainted living in the next barracks. "My wife went alone," Mr. Schultz told me. "Our eldest daughter, who was just seventeen, took our youngest, the nine-year-old. She led him to East Berlin and then across the border. Our eleven- and fourteen-year-olds went together. They had to walk at night and hide during the day. The whole family traveling together would have attracted too much attention.

"I was the last one to leave the house. I gathered all our personal papers and burned them in the fireplace. Then I walked through the house, through every room, touching the furniture, looking out the windows at the familiar landscape that had almost become a part of me. My father had built the house and I had been born in it. In the living room I stood for half an hour without moving, looking at my father's picture that had smiled down upon our family from above the fireplace for so many years. I didn't have a small photograph of him to take with me. It was like tearing my heart out by the roots when I finally turned my back and walked outside.

"Pulling the key from my pocket, I started to lock the door, when I realized how ridiculous it was. I threw the key inside on the floor, shut the door, and left. I never looked back."

"I can understand others fleeing to the West . . . but for a Christian. . . ." I struggled to find the right words to ask him if he knew that he had run away from his Christian duty, afraid to criticize him as bluntly as I had other escapees more nearly my age.

"It was for our children's sake," he said quickly, emotion mounting in his voice. "My wife and I could bear it, but we had to consider our children. I know you think we should have stayed to tell others about Jesus, and we would have if it had only been the two of us. But our children—we couldn't allow them to be raised under a system that does everything it can to force atheism on its citizens. It's going to be hard making a new start here, but at least we'll be free to believe what we want to believe, and the children won't be tempted to deny their faith in order to get an education or a job."

The stories the refugees told me of injustice and oppression, coupled with the obvious desperation that had driven them to exchange everything they had for freedom, brought back memories of the occupation of my own country during the war. Those traumatic days had slipped, like a dream, into the misty past with the rest of my childhood. It was so easy to forget. But now I was faced again with the inhumanity of man to man. The stark reality of human suffering struck me as forcibly as a hard blow to the face each time I walked through those crowded barracks and looked into faces and eyes that said more than words could ever express.

Deeper implications of my newfound relationship to God through Jesus Christ began to stir within me as I struggled to understand the teaching of Christ in the context of the world as I was beginning to see it. Already I had ceased to think of Christianity as a form or ritual to be acted out in a church. But now, for the first time, I began to think of it as a revolution—that Jesus Christ had not come to establish a religion, but to take over this world. Dimly at first, but with growing clarity and conviction, I came to believe that until *He* ruled this world there could be no real peace or justice. That His kingdom could not be established through social reform, new political programs, or ideologies—much less through war— seemed obvious. It was within the heart of each man that Christ must reign. He had not come to raise an army to contend in fields of battle, or to form a new religious organization that would negotiate compromises and treaties with nations. His call was to individuals to give Him their hearts, to follow Him alone, to come and die with Him, to accept in His death the end of their own lives. Out of this death a new world of resurrected men would arise, to live new lives under Christ's control, to form a new society—God's kingdom—as different from every earthly kingdom or human dream of Utopia as light is from darkness, as truth is from a lie.

Revolutionary? I could scarcely contain my excitement as I began to catch the vision of Christ's remedy for a race of men once made in the image of God but now twisted and deformed by self-interest and enslaved by their own ungodly egos. It was a revolution that would conquer men's hearts through divine love incarnate and would do what no other revolution could do—bring peace and righteousness to reign in men's hearts on earth.

But when I thought of the church—wasn't she supposed to be the embodiment of all He taught?—my heart sank. Where were the revolutionaries, the men who were willing to die—indeed, who had already given up their own lives so that Christ could live in them? And the youth group? We were no better. Our visits to the refugee camp had become mechanical, a conditioned response triggered each time the calendar flipped to Sunday. Our Bible studies were not producing life, but pride in our accumulating knowledge of doctrine. The social had become more popular than the spiritual. Honest reflection forced me to admit that we were more enthusiastic about entertaining ourselves than laying down our lives for others, which I was now convinced Christ demanded from all who dared to be His followers.

Similar convictions were forming within the heart of another young man in the youth group. We confessed to one another how far short of the standard Christ had set we each felt ourselves to be. Refugees by the tens of thousands were leaving everything behind to flee from East to West, giving up their former lives to find new ones. Could the cost be any less for those who would flee from Satan's kingdom into God's? Christ had said that in order to be His follower a man must forsake all. We began to spend hours together in prayer, and on our knees we pledged to Christ that we would hold nothing back, be it possessions, friends, our own lives, if only He would lead the way.

Almost without realizing what had happened, our prayers took on a definite direction. We found ourselves weeping for Hamburg, for Germany—East and West—and for the world. A passion for Christ's kingdom began to consume us. Our prayer times together became more frequent, grew longer, more tearful and intense, until our lives became one loud, sobbing, ceaseless cry to God for revival.

Revival? I scarcely knew what it meant, only that it was desperately needed and must begin in me. From somewhere came the realization that revival is the work of God's Spirit, and I began to pray that God would fill me with His Holy Spirit.

There came a night when my friend and I suddenly *knew* that revival was coming. God's Spirit would soon begin something new in Hamburg. Our hearts overflowed with this joyful certainty and yet, bicycling home through the dark streets late that night, I found myself suddenly seized by a sickening fear: Revival was coming and no one was ready! I became distraught with apprehension, afraid that my friend and I hadn't known what we were asking, that we were too young to pray for revival, that the church was unprepared, that no one would know what to do.

The verse kept going through my mind: The child has come to birth, and there is no strength to bring it forth. Helplessly panic-stricken, I saw young people believing, wanting to follow Christ—and then, lacking teaching, becoming uncertain, turning from Him, denying the faith.

Rushing into my small room, I fell upon my knees beside the bed and sobbed out to God my unpreparedness and unworthiness. "Oh, God!" I cried, "I can no longer struggle on in my own strength. You must be the one who does the work through me. I *must* be filled with Your Holy Spirit! You must possess me totally. I give myself to You. Take me and fill me to overflowing. Win others through me. Give me that power to witness for Christ that You gave to the disciples at Pentecost!"

I felt that I wasn't asking for something extra but something essential, something vital that had been missing in my life. A sense of peace, of calm and confidence, came over me. Once again my heart filled with joy. My fear was gone. Of course I wasn't ready for revival, and never would be. But God would fill me with His Spirit, so that He could do new and wonderful things through even me.

Hours passed as moments upon my knees, so real was my communion with God. He was there in the room with me. I could feel His presence, and my heart leaped for joy. But what was that strange language? It flowed from my lips, but I couldn't understand a word. I had been praying in Danish. Perhaps if I tried German—but still the unintelligible words came out when I spoke. In my Bible reading to that time nothing about speaking in tongues had ever caught my attention. Nor had I heard of Pentecostals, or a charismatic movement. I only knew that God had touched me in a new way, that He had filled me with His Holy Spirit at last.

I looked at my watch. It was 4:00 A.M.! "No wonder I can't pray sensibly," I thought. "I've been up all night! I'm so tired that I can't pray in either Danish or German. I'm too exhausted to even speak, and that's why these strange sounds are coming out of my mouth when I try. God will forgive me if I don't pray any longer."

Pulling off my clothes, I crawled exhausted into bed and fell immediately into a sound sleep.

About six o'clock I awakened, feeling as refreshed as though I had enjoyed a full night's rest. Driven by an overpowering urge to tell others about Christ, I dressed hurriedly and went out. There, coming down the side-walk toward me, I saw an elderly man, whom I had tried to witness to several times but without any success. In my excitement I forgot that he had never been interested before. "I want to tell you about Jesus!" I exclaimed enthusiastically as soon as he came near.

Immediately he began to weep, confessing his sins, calling upon Christ to forgive him.

Later as I spoke to others about Christ's death for us, the same words I had used before now seemed to carry a new power. I accepted this as an answer to my prayer.

Friends began to experience this also, and an air of openness to the gospel seemed to have settled upon Hamburg. Not that large masses were being converted—but revival had definitely begun in our youth group. There was a new love for one another, a new sense of urgency and reality, and suddenly we were all leading people to Christ wherever we went.

At our next youth meeting, there were twice as many present as before. Soon we couldn't squeeze everyone into the home where we met, and prayer groups began to spring up all over Hamburg! Every spare moment of my time was now taken up traveling on my bicycle to these new and growing groups throughout the city. I began to mark their locations on a map, and soon discovered that in every district of Hamburg God had provided a prayer group—without planning or organization. It was as though an organism, created and nourished by the Holy Spirit, had suddenly sprung up to bring new life throughout the city.

That was my first, small glimpse of what God could do if we desire with all our hearts to let Him work through us. A fire was now burning within me. The business world had lost its appeal. I knew that God was calling me to follow on another path. Soon He would open the door to a ministry that He had planned and would reveal in His time.

9

Finding the Life

Reaching the age of thirty is often a traumatic experience. Saying good-bye to the twenties forever, one suddenly feels that old age is not just for others and not as remote as once it seemed. Back in Denmark again and approaching this special age, additional considerations troubled me. Ever since that unforgettable night of prayer and blessing in Hamburg, I had known that at the age of thirty I was to step out into a life of total service to God.

That the Lord would keep me so busy thereafter that I would have no time for secular employment gave me no concern so long as I had been single. But I was familiar with the Scripture that says: He who does not provide for his family is worse than an infidel. After my marriage to Ninna, I had gone back to work in the business world in order to support her and the children that soon began to arrive at two-year intervals. And now that I was almost thirty, how would I support my family if I quit my job as the Lord had told me to?

"It doesn't make sense to quit a good job, unless I have a *reason*," I said to Ninna one day, more to check her reaction than anything.

"God has told you to. Isn't that reason enough?" came her quick response.

"But I mean. . . I don't know what I'm to do after that!"

"Yah, yah," she said, pretending to be very solemn, but unable to hide that irrepressible sparkle in her eyes. "There are diapers to change, and dishes, and laundry. . ."

"That's what God is calling me to do when I reach thirty?" I interrupted.

We both laughed, and I hugged her. It was so good to have a wife like that. If God said it, then Ninna was willing for me to do it. She was the only Christian in a family of thirteen. Her brothers and sisters had taken advantage of her after she became a believer because they knew she wouldn't complain. They often tested her to see how much of their work she would do. She had borne the teasing and injustice patiently and without bitterness, and her faith in Christ had only grown stronger.

After my thirtieth birthday, I handed in my resignation where I worked, offering to stay on another four or five months until someone could be hired to replace me. My boss was unhappy—and pessimistic—certain that it would be at least six months before he could find the right man, and he wasn't going to let me go until then. Ninna and I were praying that God would show us His will by bringing the right person quickly.

Within two weeks the perfect replacement had been hired, giving me ample time to train him. The last day of my job came and went. And that was that. In faith I had burned my bridges behind me, with no idea what would happen next.

The following morning I awakened early and spent a long time in prayer, happy, trusting God, reminding Him that now I was free from secular employment and waiting for His orders. Shortly after breakfast the phone rang. It was long distance. The caller, who had no idea that I had just quit my job, wanted to know if I might possibly be available immediately to hold a series of meetings in northern Denmark. When I put down the phone, Ninna and I knelt together to thank God for this evidence that we were in His will.

From that very day, I was suddenly so busy that it would not have been possible to hold a secular job, and it all happened so effortlessly and with such perfect timing. Then came the call to a pastorate in Jutland. As we prayed, Ninna and I felt the assurance that this was another step in God's plan for our lives. It was while pastoring that church that I first learned of the shortage of Bibles in Romania, and founded the mission under my board of elders to help meet this need.

I began to feel more and more the necessity, not just to mail Bibles, but to make personal contact with Christians in the East. My church, however, objected, feeling the mission had accomplished its goal. Unless I could find a new board in another church—and soon—the work of the mission would die. There was no thought of setting up an organization outside a local congregation.

At that very time, the elders of a congregation in Copenhagen—the largest free church in Denmark—began to express a growing interest in the mission, especially after the Bulgarian pastor, for whom I had interpreted throughout Denmark, had spoken there. So the mission was moved to the Copenhagen church, and five months later I became the assistant pastor there. This church showed a great concern for helping the believers behind the Iron Curtain and began to supply volunteer workers for this work from its large membership. One of the members of this church, Bent Jacobson, became the treasurer and soon was traveling to the East. This was also the church of Rene Hartzner, the friend who accompanied me on my first visit to Eastern Europe.

As always, when a new step had to be taken, Ninna encouraged me to trust God. Her simple, uncomplicated faith was a great inspiration, and I was to need it far more in the years ahead than I realized in those early days. Her faith would soon be severely tested, and in a way that neither of us could have imagined.

For both Rene and me, that first trip was a life-changing experience. We thought we knew so much about trusting God and following His leading, but discovered that in actual fact we knew almost nothing. It was only God's grace making up for our lack of experience that prevented us from bringing serious trouble to some of the members of the underground church and disaster upon ourselves. I have already related how and why God delayed our plane going into Sofia. There were many other similar instances of His amazing intervention to protect us and our contacts.

Early one morning, in a large Bulgarian city, Rene and I were trying to locate a very godly elderly woman who was in touch with many believers, both in the registered and underground churches. We were carrying a large sum of money, part of which was for her, but most of which she would distribute to others in difficult circumstances because of discrimination and persecution.

We had taken a cab from our hotel and driven around town like typical tourists seeing the sights—a perfect way to locate addresses that we would visit later. Confident that we were not being followed, we left the cab. After walking about a mile, we arrived finally in front of a large apartment building that bore the proper address.

"This fits the description," I said hopefully.

"Then let's go in!" Rene acted upon his own advice, and I followed him through an open door. In the dim light of the narrow hallway, we vainly tried to decipher the names on the mail slots under a wooden stairway that led to the upper floors. None of the names looked remotely like the one we had been given. I knew that often there was more than one family living in an apartment, and thought that might be the explanation.

"I'm sure this is the place," I whispered, not feeling as confident as I tried to sound. Rene gave me a look that said he hoped I had remembered the address correctly. "Never mind the names," I suggested. "She lives in apartment seven. We just have to find that."

Mounting the stairs, we began a floor-by-floor search for apartment number seven, trying to walk quietly, not knowing what we would say if someone should step out into the hallway and ask us what we were doing. Some apartments had numbers and others didn't—or else we missed them in the semi-darkness—and there seemed to be no rational sequence in the numbering that we could discover.

"Here's number seven!" whispered Rene suddenly.

"I don't think that's it," I said cautiously. "Let's look farther."

On the top floor we discovered another number seven. After consulting with one another in confused whispers, we retraced our steps through the entire building. This time we found a third number seven!

"Didn't they tell you which one it was?" demanded Rene softly as we stood in the hallway outside the number seven on the top floor.

"Nothing was said about there being more than one!" I whispered back. "But this one seems to fit the description that I memorized—'just under the attic.' "

"Why didn't you say so!" exclaimed Rene, forgetting to whisper in his excitement. "This has to be it. What are we waiting for—an engraved invitation?" He stepped toward the door, raising his hand to knock. I grabbed his arm.

"Wait a minute!" I whispered, putting a finger to my lips. "Not so loud. Look! Over there! Another stairway. Maybe there's *another* number seven up there."

"Your instructions say 'just under the attic'—not *in* it," Rene objected impatiently.

I shrugged. "Who knows what they call an attic in Bulgaria? Come on. We've got to at least look."

Even before we reached the top of the stairs, I knew

Rene was right. No one would be living up here. But I had an uncomfortable feeling about knocking on that door, and didn't know any other way to relieve it than to explore every other possibility.

Pausing on the top step, with Rene on my heels, I turned slowly around to survey the attic, and found myself looking into the surprised face of a man in his early thirties who appeared to be working up there. Fighting an impulse to turn around and run, I breathed a quick prayer. "Can you help us?" I asked in German.

"What are you looking for?" he replied guardedly, eyeing us with evident suspicion. At least he spoke something besides Bulgarian!

Sending up another quick prayer, I decided to mention our contact's name. It was dangerous, but I still had an uneasy feeling about knocking on the door and could think of nothing else to do. I had to trust the result to God.

"We're looking for a Mrs. Rumachik," I said cautiously. "Do you know where we can find her?"

He shook his head. Turning, I said quietly in Danish to Rene, "Let's get out of here! Thank God at least he doesn't know her." We began a hurried and disorderly retreat down the stairs.

"Wait!" I heard him yell after us. "Come back!"

Then I remembered. In Bulgaria the sign for *no* is nodding the head. Shaking it means *yes*. We climbed back up, and he met us at the top of the stairs, smiling.

"She's my mother. Are you from the West?"

I nodded—then remembered, and shook my head. "And you must be George!"

"No, I'm not George." There was a puzzled look on his face. "Why did you think that?"

Suddenly I was afraid. I had been told that her son George was a Christian. Suppose this one was not—and was, perhaps, even an informer!

"Why did you want to see my mother?" the man ventured.

I gave a vague, noncommittal reply, and dropped the name of the Bulgarian pastor who had visited Denmark into the middle of the sentence to see how he would react.

His face lit up and he hugged us both. "You're Christians! Praise the Lord!"

"Does your mother live in number seven on the next floor down?" asked Rene curiously.

"Yes, but I hope you didn't inquire about her there!" he added quickly, a worried expression suddenly clouding his face.

"We were just about to," I replied, "and we would have if we hadn't found you up here."

A look of relief came over him. "Praise God!" he exclaimed again. "The Lord kept you from doing it. The secret police moved a woman in to live with her. She watches that door day and night. It would have been very bad!"

"Do you live with her?" I asked.

"Oh, no! I live on the other side of town. It's a miracle I happened to be here. I stored some things up here a few months ago, and this morning I decided to come by and get them. I guess the Lord decided it. It's the grace of God!"

We didn't dare to spend much time with him. Briefly explaining our mission in whispers, we gave him the money and papers we had brought for his mother. After another hug, we hurried back down onto the street.

"Incredible!" Rene kept repeating as we walked toward a square where we could catch another cab back to our hotel. "Incredible! We wander around like two lost lambs in a den of wolves and still God makes it all work out!"

"Not just for our sakes," I reminded him. "How God got both us and him there at the same time..." I ran out of words.

"And in an attic," said Rene, "where no one would see us!"

Later that afternoon as we drove in a cab to another

part of the city, we were still talking about the amazing ways God seemed to watch over His church in the East. Following a pattern that by now had become familiar to us, we left the cab once again about a mile from our destination, then walked the rest of the way, pausing to look in store windows, once separating and rejoining a few blocks later, to be certain that we were not being followed. Eventually we came to a poor section on the outskirts of town, where we expected to find the home of a former Baptist pastor.

For courageously disregarding police "suggestions " intended to regulate his sermons, this pastor had been placed in prison. Upon his release, the government had rejected his application for renewal of his license as a pastor. The only job he could find was to sweep the streets, although he was a highly skilled and experienced engineer and spoke fluent English, French, German, Romanian, and Russian in addition to his native Bulgarian. Since these talents were all in short supply in his country, it was obvious that the government was willing to pay dearly in its campaign to suppress Christianity.

Rene and I had been warned that he lived in very poor circumstances, but we were not prepared for what we saw when we reached his house. The roof had collapsed in several places, and there was only one room that appeared to be semilivable.

"The government won't allow him to make any repairs," I explained as we came up to the front door. I was almost afraid to knock for fear the whole house would fall in.

Standing back a few feet, staring at the house in astonishment, Rene let out a long, low whistle. "I'm not going inside, even if he invites us!" He stepped closer and cautiously examined a portion of the structure next to the front door that seemed ready to buckle. "I'd be afraid this thing would collapse around my ears!"

There was no response to my gentle knock. As I tried

again, a little louder, we heard a voice calling to us in
Bulgarian. Turning around, we saw an elderly man with
a cane. He was yelling and motioning to us. Hoping he
might be a source of information, we joined him on the
dirt street.

"Sprechen Sie Deutsch?" I tried. He nodded his head. This
time I remembered it meant *no*.

"Do you speak English?" A blank look. *"Parlez-vous
Francais?"* A shrug of the shoulders, and a perplexed
expression. There was no use trying Danish.

I looked at Rene helplessly. We pointed to the house.
"Kayukov?" I asked with a questioning inflection.

He shook his head vigorously (meaning yes) and set off
with a limp down the street, motioning with his cane for
us to follow.

"Do you really think he's taking us to Pastor Kayukov?"
Rene asked skeptically.

"Kayukov?" I asked the old man again, pointing in the
direction we were going.

"Kayukov nyet," he said, pointing back at the house, and
shaking his cane as though to indicate that Kayukov
wasn't there. Then he set off again, motioning to us to
follow, all the while speaking rapidly in Bulgarian. The
one word I thought I understood was *police*. It sounds
nearly the same in many languages.

"Politsia?" I asked, pointing in the direction he was leading us and trying not to look disturbed.

He shook his head. *"Da, da,"* and a torrent of Bulgarian words with accompanying motions followed.

"Either Kayukov must have moved," suggested Rene,
"or he's been arrested again—or something—but this guy's
taking us to the police because he thinks they can tell us
where to find him. Are we just going to follow like sheep
to the slaughter?"

"I don't know what to do," I responded helplessly,
"except to pray that the Lord will stop him before we get

there. It wouldn't look good for us to be afraid to go to the police."

The old man was making good time in spite of being lame. In about ten minutes, during which Rene and I were praying fervently, we came out of the residential district into a small square. On the sidewalk in front of a large store that typically appeared to have little to sell, a man of about forty was sitting under an umbrella selling lottery tickets. When the old gentleman saw him, he seemed to get a sudden inspiration. His face brightened and he led us across the square to the lottery table, where he talked rapidly in Bulgarian to the vendor. As we waited, the latter turned and spoke to us in English.

"Are you looking for Kayukov?"

"Yes, we're friends of his," I replied quickly, which was true enough, although we'd never met him. "We're passing through and wanted to say hello to him."

"He's working now. Let's see, today's Tuesday." He pursed his lips, thinking. "I know his schedule; he's very punctual. He'll be sweeping in this square at 4:30 P.M. He's done with work at 5:00 P.M. If you can come by here then, I'll tell him to wait for you."

I told him we would, and thanked him. Our conversation had taken no more than two minutes, yet already about thirty people had gathered around to listen, some of them standing on tiptoe, curiously observing us over one another's shoulders. As we left, the crowd surged forward, babbling in Bulgarian, apparently demanding the full details from the lottery vendor.

It was about 3:00 P.M., so we decided to wait in a nearby park that we had noticed while in the taxi. There we found a bench partially hidden behind a hedge and sat down to wait.

"We'd make *great* spies," said Rene sarcastically. "I feel like the complete fool walking around with this bright red suitcase." He shoved it further under the bench with the toe of a shoe, and glanced apprehensively over his shoulder again, but we seemed to be alone in our corner of the park. The suitcase, filled with clothes for Pastor Kayukov, had been given to us by a mission on our way through Austria. We hadn't wanted to offend them by objecting to its bright color.

"It is rather conspicuous," I admitted. "But maybe it was a stroke of genius. No one would suspect us of being up to anything secretive while we're carrying *that.*"

"They might arrest us as escapees from an insane asylum!" Rene commented dryly. Suddenly we both burst out laughing as the absurdity of the situation struck us. We had carefully dressed in old, dark, shabby suits in order to keep from attracting attention—but the suitcase was so large, and such an unusually bright red, that we might just as well have been carrying a sign that read, "Hey, everybody, look at us!"

The laughter seemed to dissolve our tension, and our thoughts went back to the square. We both seemed to be thinking of the same thing. "Can you believe that they sell lottery tickets in a Communist country!" exclaimed Rene.

"Not unless I'd seen it with my own eyes," I replied.

"Anyone who wins automatically turns into a capitalist!" Rene was thinking out loud. "I'm sure they don't give them a Lenin prize instead of money. That's so contrary to everything the 'revolution' was supposed to stand for that it's even more conspicuous than our red suitcase!"

Arriving back at the square shortly before 5:00 P.M., we joined a group of people lined up at a bus stop, and looked around for the pastor.

"Hey! There he is, I bet!" whispered Rene in Danish, without pointing.

I followed his gaze to the other side of the square, and saw a man who seemed to be dressed in patches bending over, gripping one end of a large handleless push broom and deftly making long sweeping motions as he moved quickly along the gutter. Across the square, over the sounds of shuffling feet and murmuring voices, interrupted now and then by the louder noises of a passing car, came the strains of a song he was singing as he worked. I was sure it would be a hymn.

We watched in astonished fascination until at last he straightened up wearily, and, rubbing the small of his back with one hand and carrying the handleless broom with the other, walked over to stand near the lottery vendor. We could see him looking around, obviously watching for us.

Crossing the square in front of him, I was sure he saw us. I turned onto a street about fifty yards away and looked back—I could see that he was moving in our direction. We slowed our pace, and soon he overtook us.

"Follow me! I'll take you to a place where we can talk," he said rapidly in flawless English as he passed, keeping his gaze straight ahead. We followed at a safe distance, as he circled around and led us back to the park, and then, to our amazement, sat down on the same bench where we had spent the afternoon. There was no one within sight when we joined him.

The smile on his face seemed actually to glow as he greeted us warmly. We introduced ourselves and told him we had some money and clothes, and that we also brought love and Christian greetings from believers who were praying for him.

"I'm sorry about the color of this suitcase," I apologized as I slid it over in front of him. He dismissed my anxiety with a wave of the hand and thanked us.

Rene and I had both expected to find a man marked by misery and bitterness. There was reason enough: the prison terms he had endured, the loss of his pastorate, the humiliation and insult a qualified engineer who could speak six languages fluently must feel at being forced to sweep the streets . . . and on top of all of this, the loss of the wife who could no longer endure the persecution, the long imprisonments, the horrible living conditions, the discrimination and psychological pressures, the sense of shame.

Yet sitting beside him on that bench, I was sure I had never looked into a happier face. He was radiant with the joy that Christ gives to those who trust and obey—a man whose one ambition was to tell his countrymen about Jesus Christ, and to let God's love be revealed through his life.

Rene was unable to contain his curiosity. "Did you break the handle of your broom today—or lose it?" he asked.

"No. That's part of the price I pay," he replied with a shrug, obviously unwilling to talk about his troubles. He pointed upward suddenly and asked, "Do you think He's coming soon?"

If someone had asked me that in Denmark, I might have waxed eloquent and showed off my knowledge of prophecy and current world events. But with this man, I felt unworthy to speak. "What do you think?" was all I could reply.

That perpetual smile broadened into a laugh. Clapping his hands together, he leaned back and looked up into the cloud-studded sky. He didn't speak. There was an ecstatic expression on his face that said it all.

At last I broke the silence. "You've suffered so much, we can't even begin to comprehend it—what it's like living under communism."

"I'm not opposed to communism," he replied quickly. "The Bible tells us to obey the government. But my duty to God comes first. I must have the right to be a Christian...."

"And a human being!" interrupted Rene, eyeing that worn, handleless broom between his feet.

"To be a Christian is the only way to be truly human," said our friend. There was a quiet power in his voice, the ring of authority of a man who was not talking ideas but had proved in life the reality of what he said.

"Wasn't man created in God's image?" he asked. We nodded. "That image—true humanity—is restored through Christ. I *know* it for *sure!*" There was a faraway, contemplative look in his eyes. I wondered what he was seeing—mock trials, prison, torture, an empty home. But he was smiling.

He rose to go. We embraced one another fervently. There was a meeting he had to get to, but it would be too dangerous for us to come.

Rene and I sat down on the bench once more. He had asked us to wait ten minutes before leaving. We followed him with our eyes. Bright red suitcase in one hand, worn, handleless push broom in the other. Pastor, linguist, engineer, outcast, tramp—to us, he was none of these. He was a saint, a miracle of God's grace, a flesh-and-blood proof of the resurrection. We had been acutely aware that Christ was living in this man.

When he was out of sight, we looked at one another. There were tears in our eyes. I was too choked to talk. At last Rene spoke.

"I think I'm beginning to see what the Christian life really is!" He sounded as though he were talking to himself more than to me. "I wanted to be some special kind of Christian, better than all the rest at our church. So I went to Bible school. When I returned, thinking I knew so much, and the elders didn't use my talents, I turned my back on those people. I got hard. And I expected to see the same bitterness in this man, only worse. He's suffered so much more. I drew a picture of him in my mind—unhappy, broken, miserable, bitter. Instead, I feel as though I've just met Christ!"

I still couldn't speak. Rene was shaking his head. "I'll never be the same," he said quietly. "I'll never be the same!"

10

Witnessing—Eastern Style

On that first trip, during the short time that Rene and I had spent with Sonya, the girl who guided us to the homes of the two pastors in Sofia, we had tried to learn as much from her as we could about conditions in Bulgaria. We were particularly curious about how Christians were able to witness when the government forbade what it called "religious propaganda." She seemed eager to tell us.

"There are many different ways. The main thing is through our lives. Often we are asked how we can be so happy, unselfish, patient, kind."

"But suppose no one comes to you and asks," I said. "Then how do you take the gospel to your countrymen?"

"It depends how the Holy Spirit leads us. There's no formula. We must be wise as serpents and harmless as doves. Sometimes we're very bold. We're not afraid to go to prison, if it's God's will. Sometimes the Lord gives us subtle, even clever ways of spreading the Good News."

"Could you give us some examples?" Rene asked eagerly.

"Well, for instance, two sisters in Christ may go to the

park to witness. Perhaps they see a lady sitting on a bench alone, maybe with a baby in a carriage, or she's watching her children playing nearby. One of the Christian women will sit down beside her on the bench, say nothing, and start to read a newspaper, or just close her eyes for a nap in the sun. A few minutes later the other Christian, acting as though she's just walking through the park, will come and sit on the other end of the bench. She looks around and begins to exclaim to no one in particular about how beautiful the sky is, the trees, the flowers, the grass.

"Then the sister who got there first will say something like, 'Yes, isn't it marvelous how God created all these things and gave us the capacity to enjoy them!' The second woman will pretend she doesn't believe in God, ridicule the idea, and scold the other one for not being a good atheist as every Communist citizen should be. These two Christians, pretending not to know one another, will then carry on a discussion, one of them expressing the very best atheistic arguments the state always uses in its anti-religious propaganda. Then the other one will show how foolish these ideas really are.

"The conversation will be so interesting that the third woman won't be able to keep out of it. It may be possible to explain the problem of sin and why Christ came, or this may just be a first step. The three of them may even arrange to meet at that bench—or in one of their homes—at another time to carry on the discussion."

Rene and I were both fascinated. We had never heard of anything quite like this before. It sounded perfectly adaptable to our own country. "Can you give us some other examples?" I asked.

Sonya smiled patiently. "What kind of things would interest you? Let me see. Well, here's something. In town one day I suddenly noticed a woman coming down the sidewalk toward me. It was a cold day and there was ice. There was no special reason why I should have noticed her instead of others, but I seemed to see her through the eyes of Christ. He loved her so much, but she didn't know it, and He wanted me to tell her.

"So I prayed, 'Lord, make her fall down right next to me.' Just as we were passing each other on the sidewalk, she slipped on a patch of ice. Because I was expecting it, I was able to catch her, but she had twisted her ankle, and now it was difficult for her to walk. She wasn't very young, and looked rather frail, so I took her arm and helped her home. She couldn't understand that a stranger would help her like that, and asked me why I was so kind. I told her that it was because Christ was living in me, and I was then able to explain the gospel to her.

"That reminds me of another woman I met on the street. A very interesting case. I had just come out of a market where I had spent my last money for some groceries. This woman was looking in the window with a longing expression. Two small poorly clothed children were clinging to her. They looked so pitiful and hungry, that I was overcome with compassion for them, and gave her my bag of groceries."

"Were you able to tell her about Christ then?" I asked, positive that she must have.

"No, I just gave her the groceries. She thanked me, and left. At home I fell upon my knees and prayed for her. The more I prayed, the more I knew that God wanted me to help her again, to give her some other things. But I didn't know where she lived. A few days later I saw her walking through town alone and followed her to her home, without letting her see me. About a week after that, while I was praying, I felt that I must take her some shoes. So I went to her house, knocked, and when she came to the door I gave them to her.

"She looked surprised, but thanked me and took them. I didn't say anything to her, just gave her the shoes. That's all the Lord wanted me to do. A few days later, the Lord impressed upon me to bring her a child's warm sweater.

I took that to her house, but still didn't say anything to her about Christ—just gave it to her and left. Shortly after that God told me to bring her some handkerchiefs. So I did. Then one day, in prayer, I knew I was supposed to buy her some underwear at the store. It had to be brand-new.

"I took that to her house. When she opened the door and saw me there with another package, she seemed angry, but she took it again. When she looked inside and saw what it was, she began to cry and started to scold me. 'Why do you come over here at night and look in the windows and listen to what my husband and I argue about?' she demanded.

"Of course I didn't know what she meant, and asked her why she thought that. She told me that her husband was a heavy drinker, and used all the money he earned for alcohol which was why they were so poor. One day, running to jump onto a streetcar that was already moving she stepped out of one of her shoes. She couldn't jump off again quickly enough and she never found the shoe. That was her only pair. That night she pleaded with her husband to give her some money to buy shoes. He was drunk as usual and gave her nothing but curses. The next morning I brought her those shoes, and they fit perfectly.

"Then her eldest child had started school but had no sweater. It was getting colder and finally she begged her husband for money for a sweater. He refused as usual, and the next morning I brought a child's warm sweater to her. She and all the children had colds, and she begged futilely for a little money to buy some handkerchiefs. The next day I brought the handkerchiefs.

"So after telling me that, she said, 'If you weren't peeking in the windows and listening to what we said, then who tells you to bring these things—just when we need them?'

" 'God tells me,' I said to her."

"What about the underwear?" Rene and I both asked

at once, wondering what could be the story of that.

Sonya laughed. "She hadn't told me about that yet, and I was curious like you are and asked her. She said that she had applied for a job the previous day so she could earn some money to buy the things they needed. She had been hired, but before she could start she had to have a physical examination. Her underwear was so old and ragged that she was ashamed to go to the doctor's office. She had pleaded with her husband just the night before I bought the underwear to give her money to buy some, but he swore at her and told her she was too proud and that the things she had were just as good as his."

"Did she become a Christian?" I asked eagerly.

"Yes, she did. And now her husband is becoming interested, and we know he's going to be saved soon, too."

It was a tremendous inspiration just to listen to Sonya tell stories such as this. And as I began to travel more extensively throughout Eastern Europe, I soon discovered that in spite of all the money and time Communist governments are spending in a carefully organized campaign to make atheists of every citizen, the church is growing. Much is being accomplished through radio programs beamed in from outside. For instance, it is estimated that more than one million Russians have become Christians through the radio ministry of one dedicated man living in Austria who tapes messages for a number of different stations. But everywhere, also, the individual believers are winning their countrymen to Christ—sometimes in such numbers that the government considers it to be a major problem.

On one occasion in Czechoslovakia, my host was an educated man with a good job. He was the kind of person I imagined would have been difficult to reach with the gospel. Yet he was a new Christian. One evening he told me his fascinating story.

"I do a lot of traveling in connection with my work,"

he began. "We don't get lush expense allowances like you
Danes, so I usually stay in private homes rather than
hotels—it's much cheaper. One of my favorite places is
in a town about 300 kilometers north of here. Prices are
reasonable, the breakfast is generous, but the thing that
attracted me most was the unusual atmosphere of peace
and happiness. I always looked forward to staying with
them.

"One thing, however, I didn't like. There were texts
from the Bible on the walls in most of the rooms. I never
said anything about it because my hosts were a simple,
uneducated, rather elderly couple, and I thought they
were too old to change their minds. I didn't want to hurt
their feelings, because they had always been so kind to
me.

"But one time when I was there, about two years ago,
I was in a bad mood, and decided that although it was
okay if they wanted to believe that foolishness themselves,
it was going too far to make others look at those words
about God on the walls. Besides, it was an insult and really
a violation of the law to display religious propaganda in
a Marxist country where we're all supposed to be atheists.

"So I decided to give them a lesson in scientific materialism. 'Do you really believe in God?' I asked. Of course
they said they did. I told them how unscientific it was
in a modern age of space flight and advanced technology
to believe such myths as God creating the world in seven
days and so forth. I gave them all the arguments I'd been
taught, and scolded them for being poor citizens by
standing in the way of progressive socialism.

"It was a strange thing. They didn't try to argue or
disprove what I was saying. In fact, my arguments didn't
seem important to them. They knew God personally and
told me how real He was, how He answered their prayers
and how He had put love and peace into their hearts. It
made my arguments seem foolish, but I wasn't ready to
admit that. Then the old lady asked me if I would go to

a meeting with them that night. I tried to make excuses, but really I wasn't doing anything that evening. So finally, because they'd been so good to me, I decided to go just as a favor.

"There was nothing intellectual about the sermon, but it got to my heart. In fact, from the moment I walked into that room I felt as though I were in the grip of a supernatural power, which really stunned me because I didn't believe in the supernatural. At times during that evening I felt an overpowering presence in the room that literally frightened me. The people there were all like the elderly couple—friendly, kind, and with a quiet inner strength that nothing could shake. As I talked with some of them, I knew they were in touch with God and He was real. In spite of all my arguments, that simple sermon, the faces and personalities of these quiet people, convinced me that I had been created by a God who loved me so much that He had sent His Son Jesus to die for me. But I was too stubborn to admit it.

"The old couple didn't say much on the way home, but later when the other boarders had gone to bed and we were alone, I finally confessed to them that I was now convinced they were right.

" 'Would you like to become a Christian?' they asked me.

" 'I can't afford to,' I told them. 'What would the people I work with say? I'd lose my job! And my wife! What would she do? She might denounce me to the authorities!'

" 'Well, never mind about the people you work with,' said the old woman. 'God will take care of that. The most serious thing is your wife. You leave her to me and the Lord!'

"The next morning she left by train, came right here to my home, introduced herself to my wife, and stayed here for eight days, cooking, helping with the housework, taking care of the children. When I arrived back home at the end of that trip, I found that my whole family had become believers! There was nothing left but to give my heart to Christ, too!''

On one of my trips into Russia I was standing with a friend on a main street in Leningrad, waiting for a bus. A man walking along the sidewalk stopped and asked something in Russian, and my friend talked with him for a few minutes. After the stranger had left, I asked what the conversation had been about.

''He wanted to know what bus to take to get to a certain part of the city. I told him which one and where to catch it—and then I told him something more important than catching buses.''

''What was that?'' I asked, afraid that I already knew.

''I told him that God had sent His Son Jesus Christ to die for his sins.''

I was shocked and looked around apprehensively to see if the man might already be returning with the police. ''How could you dare to talk like that to a complete stranger, right here on the street!'' I exclaimed. ''Don't you know how dangerous it is?''

''And don't you know how dangerous it is for *him*,'' he replied quickly, ''if he goes out into eternity without Christ!''

I felt ashamed. In my heart I knew that I had really been more afraid of what might happen to me than to my friend if the police arrived.

''They can put me in prison,'' he said quietly. ''They've done it before. But what is that—a few years—compared with eternity? I've determined to tell the Good News about Jesus Christ to everyone I meet!''

11

Shepherds, Wolves, and Sheep

"Not all Communists are really atheists. Did you think they were?"

I was driving through the beautiful mountain country of central Romania, taking an underground pastor to an unregistered meeting, when he suddenly made this statement. I was sure he was joking.

"Of course you're kidding me," I said cautiously, taking my eyes from the road for a moment to see if there wasn't a telltale smile on his face. He looked very serious.

"Oh, I mean it," he said. "It's true."

"I don't see how a person could be a real Communist and believe in God. Do you mean a Marxist-Leninist, or some watered-down variety?"

"A Marxist-Leninist."

"But that's founded on atheism!"

He laughed. "Of course. And who invented atheism?"

"Way back there, I suppose it was Satan."

"Yes, and while he and his demons try to persuade men to be atheists, they themselves aren't. The Bible reminds us that 'the devils believe in God and tremble.' But they hate God and fight against Him."

"But men aren't devils," I objected, "even though they often act like it."

"But Satan is the god of this world, and he's the mastermind behind the confusion, suffering, hatred, wars, and all the evil on this earth. What you Westerners think is a struggle between two human ideologies to be smoothed over by *detente* is just part of the great battle between God and Satan that is rushing to its climax."

"I'm sure Satan is using capitalists just as much as Communists, only in different ways," I said. "I've often thought of this: that the very same battle between God and Satan, between good and evil, is going on both in the East and the West—and we can be deceived into missing that by battling capitalism against communism."

"Oh, I stay out of politics—and I don't know what goes on in your country. I can't go there. But let me tell you why I know there are dedicated Communists who are not atheists."

"Please do! I want to learn all I can."

"Whenever you're arrested by the police, of course you have the right to know why. They may not tell you, or they may not tell the truth, or you may not find out until you have a 'trial' six months later. But at least you can ask. One time some years ago when I was arrested and as usual asked why, the police inspector told me, 'Because you make the people stupid. After listening to you they'll all be crazy!'

" 'Why is that?' I asked him. 'Is it because I'm a Christian and I teach them about God? Is that what makes them stupid?'

" 'Yes,' he said.

" 'Well,' I replied, 'in my opinion you Communists are the ones who are stupid!'

"Usually I don't talk that way. In fact, I had never said anything like that when I had been arrested before. He was furious and demanded to know why I said that. So I told him, 'I think it's a very stupid thing for you to spend so much money and so much time to fight against God if you are so sure He doesn't really exist. Why work so hard against nothing?'

"That was when he told me something that surprised me. 'But we believe in God, too,' he said. 'We know that God exists. But we don't love Him like you Christians, and that is why we fight against Him.'

"Do you know what I replied?"

I shook my head.

"I said to him, 'Then you are even more stupid than I thought! If you know that God exists and that He is almighty, and still you fight against Him . . . then you must be *crazy*, because surely you know that you will never win!'

"They gave me three years—no worse than before. When I was released, they told me never to preach again. But God has not given any government the authority to tell me that, so I keep preaching, as Christ commanded, even though I have to do it in secret."

Because so many of the godly pastors, like this man, have been imprisoned and lost their licenses to preach, the Communists have been able to force upon some congregations a pastor who is not really a Christian but a wolf in sheep's clothing, an agent hired by the persecutors of Christians to inform against his own congregation. When such men, through political pressure, become bishops, archbishops, metropolitans, the church through its own officials adopts ecclesiastical rules designed by the government to destroy it. For example, no baptism is allowed for anyone under eighteen, no appeals to non-Christians (called religious propaganda) even in the church, no altar calls either for saved or unsaved, no Christianity outside the church building, no religious "indoctrination" of young children, even at home by their parents.

Ground down by such satanic regulations imposed upon them by their own church hierarchy, and suffocating for lack of essential freedom, believers nevertheless crowd the few churches that are still open. This is true even though the pastor is a non-Christian hired by the government to keep the church within "legal bounds" and the services are allowed in large part to impress visitors with a pretended religious freedom. Many a tourist has been deceived in this way and returns to his own country with enthusiastic reports about the "open churches" and "liberty of conscience" in Communist countries.

On occasion, government agents have laid a trap and caught a pastor in moral sin or dishonesty. Under threat of exposure, the unwilling victim has been blackmailed into becoming an informer. Robbed of spiritual power, preaching watered-down sermons approved by the official enemies of Christ, a man like this may eventually become so deadened in his conscience that he begins to enjoy the privileges that come with playing this game of cooperation. Yet regulations may be such that the congregation is powerless to vote him out in exchange for a real man of God who would feed the flock. The government has gained *de facto* control of the church while professing separation of church and state.

Once I visited such a church in a large Romanian city because I had some contacts to make there. On this particular occasion, I brought my camera and tried to act like a tourist, hoping the pastor would invite me to give some greetings, which is often allowed for a visitor. The pastor, who could speak English, sent a note to me asking if I would like to sing a solo. I wrote back that I couldn't sing but wanted to bring a greeting from the Christians in Denmark. I was not surprised when the service ended without my being allowed to say anything.

When the pastor came down from the pulpit after the benediction, instead of going to the back of the church to greet the congregation as it left, he stood in the aisle next to where I was sitting, blocking my exit until everyone had gone. Of course he engaged me in conversation, pretending to be going out of his way to be especially friendly, but I knew his real purpose was to prevent me from having any contact with his congregation.

He had been in the West a number of times, a privilege sometimes granted those who cooperate with the destroyers of true Christianity so they can declare how free the church is under communism. He had even visited my own small country of Denmark. He slapped me on the back and said, "You live in a beautiful country—but now you have come to a *free* country! You may go anywhere you want in Romania!"

I managed to swallow the retort I would like to have given him and endured his hypocrisy, still hoping to meet my contacts outside. When everyone had left the building, he said, "Come with me now. I'd like to show you my office." Westerners visiting the few open churches in Communist countries are often herded, immediately after the service, into the pastor's study, where they are kept busy listening to propaganda about freedom of religion until all of the congregation has gone home.

"That would be nice," I replied with innocent politeness, "but first I'd prefer to go outside and look around."

Reluctantly he agreed. When we stepped outside, half of the congregation was still there, clustered in small groups, deep in conversation. I tried to converse with some of them who could speak English or German, but he stuck close beside me so that no one felt free to talk. I didn't know my contacts by sight, and under these conditions it was impossible for me to inquire about them.

In Danish I said to the friend who was with me, "You talk to him and I'll try to get away."

My friend asked a question about freedom of religion in Romania, and as soon as he began to answer, I slipped away. But I had no sooner found someone who could speak German and was just beginning to feel him out to know whether I dared ask about a person I wanted to meet, when I noticed an uneasiness in his expression. Out of the corner of my eye I saw that the pastor's wife was standing just behind me, watching and listening. The person I was talking to was obviously nervous and afraid to express himself in this "free" country.

Eventually we left without having been able to meet the people we had intended to contact there.

Later that afternoon we left our hotel by taxi to find a godly woman, living in poor circumstances, to whom our couriers periodically brought Bibles for distribution to others. I was eager to meet her and also to give her some Bibles we had with us. However, after our cab had gone a few blocks, I could tell that we were being followed. Pretending to be tourists, we had the driver show us around the city, then returned to our hotel. Quickly my friend and I walked through the lobby and out another entrance, leaving this time on foot. We hadn't gone a block before we could see a man following us.

"At the next corner you go right and I'll go left!" I suggested, hoping our "shadow" would follow my friend, who didn't have the address, so I would be free to make the contact. Instead, the agent followed me. I slowed my pace and walked along looking into stores as though I were absorbed in window-shopping. The man trailing me pretended to be doing the same, keeping a discreet distance. I timed myself to arrive at a bus stop just as the last person had climbed aboard, never taking my eyes from the store windows, watching the reflection.

Suddenly I dashed to the bus and leaped aboard just as it pulled away. Off we went, leaving my "shadow" running along the sidewalk far behind. Leaving that bus, I walked a few blocks and took another one in a different direction. Eventually I got off that one and walked the rest of the way to the address, remembering bitterly the pastor's hollow words, "Now you're in a *free* country. You may go wherever you like."

Arriving at the address, I climbed up an outside stairway as I had been instructed. Part of the attic had been turned into a tiny apartment. Standing on the top step, wondering if I had found the right place, I peeked through a window and saw a woman praying. "Thank You, Lord," I said under my breath, and knocked gently.

When she hesitantly opened the door a crack, I said softly in German, "I have Bibles for you in my hotel." She let me in quickly.

After we had talked about the Lord and His work for a few brief moments, I knew I must go. "When is the best time to bring the Bibles?" I asked.

"Come back at 11:00 tonight," she said. "Which way did you come in just now?"

"There's only one way, I guess," I replied, puzzled.

"There's a back way—a small gate through the fence on the alley. Come in that way tonight. Then the pastor who lives downstairs and cooperates with the Communists won't see you. But be careful. Now go quickly. And remember—now you must go out the way you came in. The secret police have a house just across the street, and they'll be watching to see when you leave."

Careful to see that we were not followed, my friend and I returned with the Bibles that night. This dear widow wanted to serve us something, although she was very poor. She gave us each a glass of water and a spoonful of jam on a plate. We knew it was the very best she had. I couldn't have felt more honored if I had been invited to a king's feast. What Jesus said about the "widow's mite" came into my mind, and I felt I understood in a new way.

We left that city for another town where I had an official invitation to preach in a registered church, something rarely possible today. The pastor seemed to me to be a man who desired to serve God, yet felt it was necessary to cooperate with the government for fear that if he didn't, the authorities would remove him and put in his place one of their own agents who would destroy the church.

He asked me to preach at least an hour and a half. "Tell

the people how to be saved," he suggested earnestly. "Tell them of sanctification and holiness, about baptism and discipleship—all the things I'm not allowed to preach about. You know what they are."

All chairs and benches had been removed from the church so that more people could be crowded in to stand packed closely together. The service lasted about four hours. The church was only allowed to have one service on Sunday, so they made it a long one.

That evening the pastor took me to an underground meeting held in a home. Some of the people who were in his church that morning were here, also. There is often no clear distinction between the registered church and the so-called underground church. Some believers attend both meetings, eager for fellowship with other Christians wherever and whenever they can find it.

On the way to this meeting the pastor had said to me, "I want you to promise me that we leave at half-past nine and no later."

"Of course," I had said, "I'm your guest. Whatever you want me to do, that's what I'll do."

We arrived at about six o'clock. After a meal and many lustily sung hymns, I was asked to preach. When I had been speaking for an hour or so, the people began to ask questions: "What is God's grace? Is faith a gift? What is sanctification? How does sanctification work in our lives? What is the difference between sanctification and salvation?" Some of the questions were asked out of context and betrayed a tragic ignorance of Scripture. But I knew there was good reason for this. There were only two Bibles among all those present that night. Earlier in the evening I had looked at one of them and noticed many names written inside the front cover.

"Are these the people who get to read the Bible?" I had asked.

"They are each allowed to have it for one hour a week," I had been told. "But they don't read it. They spend that time copying parts of it for themselves."

It wasn't hard to be patient with people like that when they asked childish questions or questions out of context. I thanked God for having given me the special privilege of teaching His Word to believers such as this throughout Eastern Europe, believers who had been denied by their rulers the right to have Bibles of their own. I've seen an entire Bible handwritten, but many people have only been able to copy parts of it. They don't understand the Bible well because they've never had the opportunity to read it all, much less to study it.

Sometimes I've answered questions at such meetings all night. But this time, promptly at 9:25, the pastor stood up and announced that he and I must leave.

There was a loud protest from those present. "No! You can't take him away now! We've come here with many questions!"

Nevertheless, the pastor was adamant. "I must go *now!*" he insisted.

"That's not fair! We have so much more to ask!"

"I must do it," he said firmly. "It's too dangerous for me to stay here any later than this. I could be condemned for being involved in an underground meeting as it is, and I can't stay any longer!"

Most of the people were very angry when we left. After such experiences I began to understand better some of the tensions and conflicts that often divide the believers themselves in parts of Eastern Europe. Some take a hard line and refuse to have anything to do with the official church, calling it the "synagogue of Satan." Others say they must cooperate at least to the minimal extent necessary to keep the little freedom they still have, fearing that otherwise the government would close every church as has been done in Albania and was also true in China, until the recent change in policy. It is small wonder that there are often confusing and conflicting reports in the West concerning conditions for Christians behind the Iron Curtain.

In my travels I have encountered varying shades and degrees of compromise and also learned some of the tragic reasons, which have taught me that it is not always easy to correctly appraise the situation, particularly as a visitor just passing through. The full truth will never be known until our Lord returns and judges righteously. I do not forget that I also will be judged according to my own words and deeds.

Moving on to another town, I had dinner a few days later with a well-known registered pastor. Glancing around his nicely furnished apartment with its large windows and balcony looking out upon a breathtaking view, I could not keep from contrasting his comfortable situation with that of another pastor I knew—who was at that moment sweeping gutters with a handleless broom. Cooperation with the secret police had its undeniable rewards. The physical evidence lay in the apartment about me, in such striking contrast to the acute poverty I had seen among so many underground believers.

But there was another contrast that struck me, too. The conversation around the table with this man, his wife, and son was pleasant enough, but there was something missing. The spontaneity, the deep joy and confidence, the spark of humor, the openness, the intense love and sense of comradeship I had felt among so many who were living on a fraction of his salary, was conspicuous by its absence.

When we had finished the meal, I decided to ask him about the pros and cons of working with the authorities. He certainly should know. "These reports you have to make about the members of your congregation—how much must you tell to satisfy the police?"

"Well, there's no problem about that," he replied quickly. "Don't you think Romania is a beautiful country? And such weather we've been having! Why don't we take a walk and enjoy it?" Putting a finger to his lips, he motioned for me to follow him outside.

"I can't talk about such things in my apartment," he said when we had reached the street. "I'm not sure, but they may have hidden microphones in there and are recording what I say."

As we walked through a nearby park, he poured out his heart to me. "I've spent quite a few years in prison. I'm not afraid to go back or to die for Christ, if that's His will. But I love my congregation, and I *have* to cooperate with the authorities. If I give them an excuse, they'll remove me and make one of their own men the pastor, someone who has studied theology in order to mix it with Marxism—a wolf in sheep's clothes, a God-hater wearing a cleric's collar. That would be dreadful! I couldn't bear it!"

I could feel the agony of his soul. He looked at me questioningly, but I didn't know what to say. Who was I to condemn him?

"I don't cooperate completely with them," he continued. "I make certain reports, but the information I give them means nothing. Usually. Often I hide things, but I can't hide everything. Do you understand?"

"It's difficult for me, never having lived here. How much does this restrict your ability to really be a pastor?"

We were sitting on a bench now, half-facing one another. There was a tortured expression on his face.

"Well, of course there are great restrictions. As you know, I'm not allowed to preach what I would like. I can't evangelize or have Sunday school. I have to get a permit from the government in order to baptize anyone, and I don't dare baptize very many, or those too young. Some of my congregation have been baptized secretly. It's a dreadful situation! But what can I do?"

There was a long silence. I sat there uncomfortably, not knowing how to answer him.

"Do you condemn me?" he asked at last.

I had heard such men condemned, and I had agreed

when I was safe in my own country. But now I wasn't sure. I was afraid to think what I might do under similar circumstances. I hesitated for a long time before replying.

"I love you as a brother," I said at last. "I know you love Jesus Christ, and He is the only One who can judge you. I also will stand before Him one day to give an account."

An intense inner agony seemed to reflect itself in his face. "Let me tell you, I'm a tortured man. Sometimes I think this kind of torture is worse than anything I ever had in prison. Should I stand for what is right if it means my congregation will have a Communist pastor who'll preach a mixture of theology and Marxism? What would that accomplish?"

"I understand how you feel about that," I said sympathetically. "And I don't have the answer. What would Paul or Peter do? What would Jesus do? *He* will have to give you the answer—and the courage."

He dropped his head suddenly as though he could no longer look me in the eye. "Also my son...my only son...." He hesitated—perhaps he hadn't intended to say this—then went on breathlessly like a penitent in a confessional. "My son starts high school next month. I know that if I don't do as they say, he can't have an education, and that would be worse for me than prison!"

He wrung his hands. "I keep hoping the situation will ease...that someone in the West will take up our cause ...that the United Nations...or public opinion around the world will force our leaders to..." The words floated away unfinished on the afternoon breeze. "Would you pray for me?" he asked helplessly.

As we prayed together on that park bench, I could see a picture in my mind of the millions of Christians in the West living easy, self-satisfied lives, unconcerned by the sufferings of their brothers and sisters in the East. Some of them had perhaps responded to an emotional appeal to help the church behind the Iron Curtain—responded with a monetary gift, but not with the love and concern and travailing prayer that were often more costly and more needed.

As I prayed for strength for this tortured man condemned by his own conscience for compromising his commitment to Christ, I wondered whether the church in the West, of which I was a part, had not unknowingly compromised even more.

Traveling on to Bulgaria, I found myself one Sunday in the very church where the Bulgarian refugee for whom I translated in Denmark had once been the beloved pastor. He had asked me particularly to try to give a special greeting there. No foreigner is allowed to preach from the pulpit in Bulgaria, but they allowed me to stand in the aisle and say a few words of greeting that Sunday. Since I was afraid that the pastor, if he didn't like what I was saying, might change it when he interpreted, I tried to keep him from knowing what was coming next.

"I bring you greetings from the Christians in Denmark and other countries in the West. It is said about my country that it is free, but it's really not, because we're bound by sin. The most important thing is not whether you're in a so-called free country but whether you're free yourself. 'Whom Christ sets free, they are free indeed.'

"There are some Scripture verses that express a special word of greeting better than I can. They are verses twenty-seven through thirty of the first chapter of Philippians."

The pastor read them for me from the Bulgarian Bible: "Only let your manner of life be worthy of the gospel of Christ. That whether I come and see you or else be absent, I may hear of your affairs that ye stand fast in one spirit, in one mind, striving together for the faith of the gospel; and in nothing terrified by your adversaries. . .for unto you it is given in the behalf of Christ not only to believe on Him, but also to suffer for His sake; having the same conflict that ye saw in me and now hear to be in me."

As he was reading, I remained standing in the aisle and looked around the church. Tears were beginning to run down cheeks, handkerchiefs were being pulled out to dab at eyes. By the time he had finished, many were weeping openly. I was sure they knew that this was no ordinary greeting, but a message from their beloved former pastor, who had been arrested on a trumped-up charge, tortured, and forced to make a false confession. He was now in the West but had not forgotten them.

12

$10,000—and Other Mistakes

"Number 347," I said matter-of-factly to the girl behind the desk, as she took her attention momentarily from several guests with whom she had been arguing heatedly in Bulgarian. Mechanically she reached for the key, pulled it out of its pigeonhole, and handed it to me. Taking brief note of the passport I put on the counter, she turned once again to give her attention to the small group of guests that I hoped would keep her distracted long enough. So far so good!

I was in one of Bulgaria's finest Black Sea resort hotels. As I walked down the thickly carpeted hallway toward the elevator, I found it difficult to keep from betraying to the four approaching Russian officers the elation and excitement that leaped within me. In spite of myself, my pace quickened to match the pounding of my heart. There was good cause to be excited.

I had been trying—as had others—to get into Room 347 for the past two and a half years, always without success. I had written for reservations, gone out of my way to come to this hotel, and in my letters or appeals at the front desk in person (being careful not to arouse suspicion by my unusual interest) had extolled the virtue of Room 347—its marvelous view, its proximity to the elevator, the comfortable bed, the pictures on the wall and the wallpaper itself, the evening breeze on the balcony, the pleasant memories from the past, its restful decor and "something special about it" that seemed to guarantee a sound sleep all night. Obviously I wanted this room very badly and would gladly have paid the most exorbitant price to get it, but the response to my appeals had always been the same—"occupied." Until now!

Great as the virtues of Room 347 may have been, the real reason I wanted it—a reason I hoped the hotel personnel had not yet discovered—was that $10,000 in cash lay hidden there, left by a frightened courier of another mission. This was the sum of money he had been carrying—undeclared at the border upon entering the country—when he had arrived in this town, come to this hotel, and occupied that now-famous room. His mission had been to turn the funds over to a Bulgarian in that city, who would distribute it to relatives of prisoners and other members of the underground church who were in dire need. However, each time he had ventured from the hotel to make his contact, he had been closely followed. After several unsuccessful attempts to escape his shadow, he had become too frightened to try again.

Returning to his room from the latest attempt to make the delivery of this large sum, and panic-stricken at his inability to escape the persistent two-legged bloodhounds that dogged his footsteps, he felt certain that his arrest was imminent. At any moment he expected the police to knock at the door. The one sensible thought that penetrated his confusion was: "I've got to hide the money! And quickly! But where?"

Forcing himself to forget his fear of arrest and think calmly, he began a careful but rapid inspection of the room. In the mattress? They might change that, or someone falling asleep smoking could set it on fire. Behind a picture? In a light fixture? Suddenly he noticed the metal guard on the radiator that heated the room. It was secured by two screws. He had a knife. Quickly he pulled the guard away. The radiator was set in a recess in the wall below a window. There was the place! The hole for the pipe bringing hot water out of the wall next to the radiator had been carelessly made. It was half again too large. Praying desperately, asking God to forgive his fear and watch over this money, he stuffed the large wad of bills far back into the wall on the underside of the pipe. No one could see them without bending far down. Now if the radiator would only keep working so no plumber would be nosing around, someone else could return in a week or two, recover the money, and nothing but time would have been lost.

That had been nearly three years before, and in spite of numerous attempts, no one had yet gotten a reservation for Room 347. But I had the key in my hand now, and all I wanted was five minutes alone in there. I pushed the button, and the elevator door opened.

"Sir! Wait...you at the elevator!"

Forcing myself to turn slowly, I looked around to see the girl who had given me the key, running down the hall toward me and waving my passport. The four Russian officers had stopped and turned around to watch. A man was coming out from behind the desk to hurry after her.

She ran up to me breathlessly. "Let me have that key!"

"But you just gave it to me," I said, looking as perplexed and innocent as I could.

"You're not Colonel Krakov!" She shook my passport under my nose. "That's not your room! Why did you ask for that key!"

"But you gave me the key!" I protested in an injured voice, acting offended now. "I didn't say it was my room—I don't have one yet. But I thought you were putting me in this one. Is it occupied?" I held out the key, and she snatched it.

"Of course it is! The entire third floor is occupied by a delegation of army officers from Russia! Why did you want that room?" She and the man who had joined her were regarding me with extreme suspicion now.

"A friend of mine who stayed here some time ago said it was a very nice room and recommended it to me..." I let the words come out slowly, indignantly, so they would have no doubt that I was highly offended.

The hard look wavered just a little. I held out my hand. "If you would be so kind as to return my passport, I'll go to another hotel where they treat the guests with some courtesy!"

She hesitated, looked at the man uncertainly, then dropped the passport into my hand. I walked slowly, stiffly, in a high state of justifiable pique, across the lobby, out the door...and breathed a deep sigh of relief as soon as I had reached my car. Chalk up one more failure!

A few weeks later, driving with Bent Jacobson toward Czechoslovakia, I was still chafing over my repeated failures to get the $10,000. And now after this latest episode, I wouldn't dare to try again. Why had I been so foolish as to leave my passport on the desk? The girl on duty was so preoccupied, she might have thought I was Colonel What's-his-name if I hadn't done that. But then I didn't know the room was occupied, and it's normal to show one's passport when checking in.

Fretfully occupied with such thoughts, I was surprised to see that we had reached the border so quickly. The Austrian customs officer scarcely glanced at our passports as he waved us through. Suddenly I realized, to my chagrin, that I had just made another blunder—this one worse. There was a cardboard box full of Czech Bibles sitting in plain view in the back of our nearly empty small station wagon. It was too late to hide them now! We were in the narrow strip of no-man's-land between Austria and Czechoslovakia and already under the gaze of the Czech guards awaiting us.

"Lord, forgive me for another mistake!" I prayed. "Please don't let them see that box—or take those Bibles. Not for my sake, but for the name of Jesus and the sake of His sheep who need Your Word!"

I well knew that nothing so attracts the attention of customs officials and border guards as boxes and cartons, especially as large as the one sitting conspicuously behind me now. It obviously did not contain the customary personal belongings one carries in a suitcase and demanded investigation. Yet, as I prayed continuously, the guards searched our luggage carefully, but ignored the cardboard box completely, as though they hadn't seen it. I had crossed enough borders to know that God, in His mercy, had granted us another miracle when we needed it badly. Then why not in that hotel? I had no answer for such questions.

Arriving at the home of our contact early that afternoon, we immediately put our car out of sight and disposed of the Bibles. This is always the number-one priority of the moment. The police may be notified of our presence by an informer and suddenly arrive to make a search.

We had just begun to relax when a woman burst excitedly into the apartment to tell us that a courier of another mission had been discovered and arrested. He had passed the border safely, but while traveling through the country his car was hit by a train, seriously injuring him and dislodging the Bibles from their secret hiding places. When the police arrived to investigate the accident, they found the Bibles scattered throughout the car. His arrest had set off a frantic campaign by the police to find the Bibles he had already delivered.

"This man left two hundred Bibles with the Cherneys!" my host exclaimed. "The police will find it out and search their house. We have to warn them!"

"Where do they live?" I asked.

"More than a hundred kilometers from here—and we have no car!"

"But *we* have!" Within minutes, Bent and the woman who had brought the news were in our car and on their way.

About 6:30 that evening, people quietly began to arrive for the meeting, one or two at a time, several minutes apart. Upon entering the apartment, they carefully removed their shoes and throughout the evening great care was taken to make no sounds that would betray to neighboring apartments, especially below, the presence of so many visitors.

When Bent returned late that night, the meeting was still in progress. Although we were staying several days and there would be a similar meeting every night, the questions continued until nearly four o'clock the next morning. We discussed such things as the doctrines of grace, election, predestination, baptism, sanctification. But those present were concerned most of all about the return of Christ. Did I believe His coming was near? Especially what did I think were the *signs* of His return, and could they be observed in the world today?

This is one of the questions encountered most frequently behind the Iron Curtain because, like Bibles, any literature that does not adhere strictly to the official propaganda line is under embargo. Books by Einstein, for instance, are banned in Russia because he said that the discoveries of science point to the existence of God. Western newspapers and magazines, of course, are not available. News release is under absolute government control. As every business is owned by the state, so every newspaper editor, reporter, copywriter, photographer, radio and television commentator is an employee of the government and is allowed no deviation from official dogma. Much of what happens in the world is never reported in Eastern Europe, and when it is, the story may be sketchy, slanted, and not released until weeks or months after the newsworthy event took place.

Like everyone else in such countries, Christians are

hungry for news of world events, but for a special reason. They are eager to learn whether Bible prophecy is being fulfilled in the happenings reported freely in the world press, but not in their own media. They are dependent upon sources outside their own countries to supply this information.

"What's going on in the world today that indicates the coming of Christ is near? Please take the prophecies in Daniel and Revelation and show us how current events around the world indicate that the fulfillment is near." Such questions kept us all awake into the early morning hours, when people began leaving as they had come, quietly and carefully, one or two at a time. The last ones left about four o'clock.

After a few hours of sleep and a very late breakfast, I had an opportunity to ask Bent about his trip of the evening before. "As we approached the village," he said, "there were large puddles and flooded fields beside the road. There had been a very severe storm just before we came. It had blown a huge tree across the highway just about two kilometers this side of the Cherney's house, blocking traffic. The police were there directing a big crane, and workmen were busy with power saws. Cars were backed up on both sides of the fallen tree, but our small car just squeezed under and we got through without delay.

"When we arrived at their house, the village looked deserted. I guess everyone was down watching the action. But the Cherneys were home. After putting the car out of sight in an old barn, we explained why we had come. They told us that the Lord had already warned them, and they had taken the Bibles somewhere else! One of them had had a vision—or a revelation—from which they understood that there would be an obstacle of some kind across the road keeping the police busy until they had hidden the Bibles in another place!"

"Would you dare to tell people back in Denmark about

this?" I asked seriously. "Who would believe you?"

"I don't know whether I'd believe it myself," said Bent, "if I hadn't been there. And listen to this! The woman who went with me told me that her husband had broken his arm in a fall recently. Two weeks after it was set, the doctor took an X-ray and discovered that the bone was growing crooked. He told her husband to come to the hospital the next morning so he could rebreak the bone and set it again. That night a group of believers that meet secretly in their home laid hands on him and prayed. The next morning at the hospital he begged the doctor to please take another X-ray before doing anything to his arm. Reluctantly he did and discovered that the bone was completely and perfectly healed."

Miracles do not always happen. As in the days of the early church, sometimes godly Christians are allowed to suffer in prison, and sometimes die in their cells half-starved, overworked, and tortured. God does not always choose to work through miracles, although most of us would undoubtedly experience more of His miraculous power if we were not so blinded and prejudiced by doctrinal arguments and unbelief. But the Christian life is not just floating on a pink miracle cloud. There is work and suffering and much to learn, often through mistakes.

Returning to Denmark, I found a letter waiting for me from one of our couriers describing a recent trip into Bulgaria. He had delivered most of his Bibles but had about 100 left, which he intended to take to a certain village. However, for a number of miles before reaching the village, he had noticed a car following him. One is followed almost constantly in Bulgaria, and just as in Russia, every time a vehicle passes a policeman, secret or uniformed, he copies the license plate number, and records the time, place, and date.

So our courier drove on to a large city a few miles beyond. Parking his car on the street, he took a room in a hotel. The moment he entered the room, he locked the door, took the Bibles quickly out of his luggage, and hid them under the bed. Then he distributed his clothes and personal things evenly through all the suitcases. Working rapidly, he had just finished when there was a loud knock at the door. When he opened it, several uniformed police burst in and searched his suitcases. Looking out the window, he could see other police peering through the windows of his car, which he had locked. No one looked under the bed.

The following morning he checked out of the hotel, locked the suitcases, which once again contained the Bibles, in his car, and began a tour of the city by bus. After transferring to several buses, he escaped the person who was trailing him, returned to his car and drove immediately to the nearby village. Certain that no one was following him this time, he delivered the Bibles and quickly left. The Bibles were immediately transferred to another location several miles away. Within an hour, he later learned, the police had arrived to search the house where his car had been parked—obviously seen and reported by an informer.

By this time Ninna and I knew that I had committed myself to a dangerous business. The day might come when I would not return from one of my trips—if that were God's will. Our couriers were conscious that we must walk closely with the Lord and be sensitive to His leading if we were to expect His protection. Yet mistakes could still happen—and I had an uneasy feeling when one of our couriers left for Czechoslovakia a few months later.

Through a special arrangement with Bible societies in the West, a limited number of Bibles were now being printed in Czechoslovakia. There was still a shortage, but our mission felt that it was no longer great enough to warrant the increased risk of taking Bibles across the border, especially after the secret police tightened their grip on that country following the Russian takeover. Conditions for the church had become extremely severe.

We had begun a special radio broadcast for Czechoslovakia designed to encourage the Christians there. We knew that after the relative freedom under Dubcek, the church was ill-prepared to withstand the new wave of persecution that accompanied the Russian occupation. The only way we could let the Christians in that country know of our new broadcast was to send a courier.

"Remember what your mission is," I warned the courier just before he left. "Stick to that—and don't get involved in anything else. You are to notify as many key Christians as possible of our new broadcast, and have them pass the word along—*and don't take any Bibles!*"

"But I can't go without taking at least a few!" he protested.

"Look," I said firmly, "that's not the purpose of your trip this time."

"Hans, I won't take very many. The Lord has always gotten me through before."

"I don't believe you should take *any!*"

"Just two. Okay? Suppose they find them. It won't mean that much."

"The way they've clamped down, it could mean plenty right now," I insisted. "I don't believe you should take them. But you know our policy—we don't dictate to you. If you feel the Lord wants you to, then go ahead, but be sure *He's* telling you to."

Upon his return, he came over to report to me. I was surprised to see him back so quickly. From the look of chagrin on his face, it was obvious that something had gone seriously wrong.

We sat down together in my office, and he began to tell me his story. "They stopped the train for about an hour at the border. It was swarming with police. I began to wish I had taken your advice. Two of them came into my compartment, took everything out of my suitcase, and sifted through it, examining each piece of clothing— everything! Of course they found the two Bibles.

"Believe me, Hans, they meant business. They put me under arrest and pulled me off that train so fast. . .took me in a car to an interrogation and started in on me. I mean they were rough!"

"Just for two Bibles?" I asked.

He grinned sheepishly. "Just for two Bibles. And yet the Czech government is printing Bibles—a few. It doesn't make sense!"

"They need western currency," I reminded him. "They get paid twice for those Bibles—once by the Bible societies and again by the Czech Christians who have courage enough to buy them. They have to register to get them, and a lot of Christians, as much as they would like to have a Bible, are afraid to do that. Anyway, go on with your story."

"I haven't told you the worst of it. In the middle of the interrogation, I remembered something horrible. I had memorized the names and addresses you gave me, but I had forgotten to destroy the piece of paper they were written on! It was still in my coat pocket, and I knew they would search me thoroughly before they were finished.

"When they told me to take off my coat and hand it to one of them, I managed, somehow, to get the paper out of the pocket. I started to turn up my shirt cuffs, and I put the paper, wadded tight now, in my left cuff. While one of them went through my coat, the other one started to search me. The first thing he did was reach for the cuff that had the names and addresses in it! When he pulled down my left cuff, the wad of paper fell out. I caught it with my right hand and put it into my mouth—and none of them noticed it!

"Don't ask me how, Hans. I couldn't possibly have done it and can't tell you exactly how it happened. But I had that paper in my mouth, and it was a miracle. That's all I can say."

"Did you swallow it?"

"I couldn't. It was too big. I would have choked. So I

had to soak it in saliva. Then I chewed it carefully and somehow got it down. Believe me, I knew I was eating my own words when I swallowed it!"

"Did they let you go on then?"

"Not on your life! I had one other book besides those two Bibles—a Danish-German dictionary—and they confiscated that, too! Then they took me back to the train station and saw that I got on the next train back to Germany, after telling me never to try to enter Czechoslovakia again!"

We prayed together, thanking God for the problems He allows to come our way so that we can learn the lessons He wants to teach us. We confessed that we were just finite, fallible, feeble creatures who need His guidance and protection. We thanked Him for His mercy, and especially for not letting those names and addresses fall into the hands of the police.

Our mission had three couriers working now, and from their experiences and my own, I had long since learned that we were not fighting secret police and informers, nor even atheists out to destroy Christianity, but we were in a spiritual warfare whose scope and violence staggered my imagination. I believed with all my heart that it was a ministry that God had called me to, a ministry for which we needed the power, protection, and guidance of His Holy Spirit. Nothing else would suffice.

When the news arrived that someone had at last—after three years of frustration and failure—been given a reservation for Room 347, found the $10,000 still in its hiding place, and turned it over to the persecuted believers, I was reminded again that God is in the process of molding us into the image of Christ and that sometimes even mistakes play their part. I was sure that they didn't *have* to happen, but I was grateful that I served a God who could take even my blunders and turn them into blessings. I only wished that all men knew Him and honored Him, so that His kingdom would be a reality on this earth.

13

Paralyzed for Life

Toward the end of 1969 unbelievable news came out of Russia. Maria Braun had lost her faith! At least this was the story being carried in Soviet newspapers, but I refused to accept it. Maria was an inspiration—a hero of the faith! An eighteen-year-old girl who had taught scores of children in her village about Christ in spite of the threats of a godless government, she had accepted her five-year prison term bravely, considering it a privilege thus to suffer for Christ. And now to deny Him? Impossible!

Then couriers returned from Russia with the verification. Maria's mother had visited her in prison just before her release. Maria no longer prayed and said she didn't believe in God. What a victory for atheism! Soviet newspapers began to run feature articles on the story, including Maria's own statement of her deliverance from religious myths and superstition:

> Services and fasting had broken down my health, so I was put in the hospital. I was overwhelmed that doctors and nurses would be so kind to a sick person like me, and how friendly they were to me when

they realized that I was a criminal. In 1969 I became
a nonbeliever, and soon after this I was set free. Even
before my sentence was ended the Soviets saw my
conscientious work and gave me liberty. I want to
thank all who have helped. My dear comrades, I
want to tell you how happy I am now. With horror
I remember the old days. To all parents who raise
their children, I want to say beware for your children's sakes of the sects and church people for their
influence. These "servants of the Lord" will try to
make them spiritual slaves and later it will be very
difficult to break the religious chains.

Maria's statements strongly indicated brainwashing. It
was not "services and fasting" that had broken her health.
That was perfect when she entered prison. Only after two
years was she put into the prison hospital, two years
during which she was allowed no visitors. Now she
praised the kindness of the doctors and nurses. But what
about the torture that had made her need their services?
They had done a thorough job on her "rehabilitation into
socialist society."

With bitter remorse I confessed to the Lord that I had
forgotten to pray for Maria. In the beginning I had prayed
for her daily, but I had soon forgotten. Was it because
I didn't think Maria really needed my prayers? Had I seen
so many miracles behind the Iron Curtain that I had begun
to look upon the persecuted believers there as super-
Christians who were always victorious?

Maria's "conversion" to atheism struck a shattering
blow to my own faith and raised a troublesome question.
It had taken prison and torture to break Maria, but what
about the rest of us who hadn't experienced such pressures? Could we stand up any better? Then weren't we
all "Marias" without even knowing it? I was frightened
by the thought. And how many other Marias were there

in Russia, China, Albania, Bulgaria, Romania, Czechoslovakia, ready to crack under the weight of unbearable pressures? What did the church in the rest of the world know or care about them? The spiritual battle was deeper, more vicious, and subtle than I had ever imagined. I began to wonder if I was really in the battle or just playing a game on the side.

My duties as assistant pastor at the large church in Copenhagen were keeping me occupied day and night, necessitating long hours and little sleep just to keep up with routine correspondence for the mission. The physical exhaustion was bad, but far worse was the mental strain I had felt for some time. Early enthusiasm had waned, and now some of the congregation resented the emphasis upon believers in faraway countries as an intrusion into the life of the church, diverting attention and finances from local needs and programs. Finally the pastor had told me that I must never again mention my work behind the Iron Curtain. I sensed that he had begun to wish he had never allowed the mission to come to his church. Gradually misunderstandings developed, which led to a breakdown of communications between us. As misunderstandings grew, I began to feel that the work of the mission did not belong in a local church but under a separate board.

On top of these tensions had come the news of Maria's conversion to atheism and the self-condemnation I felt for not having done all I should have for her and others in similar circumstances. Driven by a feeling of desperation because of the extreme needs of the suffering believers in the East, I asked the church board for permission to make a two-week tour of Danish churches in an attempt to arouse financial aid and prayer support for Christians in Communist countries. Although I knew my request might stir more controversy and increase the tension, I could not do otherwise. I felt compelled to challenge the

church in Denmark to reach out in love to her counter-
part behind the Iron Curtain.

Every night I was in a different pulpit, appealing for
help to be given to the underground church—not just
financial aid or the supply of Bibles but love and persistent
prayer, the kind of prayer support I had failed to give to
Maria. The response was good, but I had been pushing
myself too hard. The long hours, lack of sleep, and inner
tension had taken their toll. On my way homeward at last,
I felt on the verge of complete exhaustion.

Taking the ferry back from Jutland, I left my car below,
went into the upper lounge, and settled back in a chair.
The next thing I remember was opening my eyes to find
myself collapsed on the floor of the lounge. Several people
were bending over me, and I could hear the vessel's
loudspeaker asking if there were a doctor aboard. I opened
my mouth to speak, but no sound came out. My wallet
was in my coat pocket with all my identification in it. I
managed to point to the pocket with my left hand, after
discovering that my right side was paralyzed. A sickening
wave of panic accompanied that realization, and then I
lost consciousness again.

Later I learned that Ninna had been notified by the
ship's phone immediately. When the ferry docked, a
waiting ambulance took me to a nearby hospital. Ninna
arrived there later that night to find me still in a coma.
The doctors frankly told her that it was doubtful I would
live.

The following morning I regained consciousness. Ninna
was sitting beside my bed. I recognized her and could hear
her talking to me, but I was unable to reply. Ninna, the
nurses coming in and out, the intravenous feeding appara-
tus, the white-walled room, everything around me seemed
unreal, as though I had left the world but could still watch
from a distance. The doctors by now had diagnosed my
case as a stroke, so massive that there was no hope, but
they were doing all they could. I was transferred to a

larger hospital in Copenhagen. Ninna came with me in the ambulance, and one of the drivers followed in my car.

The day after arriving in the Copenhagen hospital, I was able to talk, but my mouth seemed to have very little connection to my damaged brain. My doctor cautioned Ninna not to become too hopeful. She tried to tell me that it was our youngest son's birthday. He was just a year old. I smiled weakly and said something incoherent about him being nineteen. Our eldest child was seven. Bravely Ninna would not allow her eyes to betray to me the despair she felt inside.

Somehow I clung to physical life. My head began to clear, but I was still paralyzed on my entire right side. After two months, I was able to sit up in a wheelchair part of the day and even managed to get around a little by pushing it with my left hand. I was able to do little more than read, pray—and think. I chafed under the inaction and the helplessness I felt. Unaware of the doctors' prognosis, I dreamed of the moment I would be healed and working for the Lord in Communist countries once again.

During most of my waking hours my mind flipped restlessly through the pages of the past, going over my experiences in Eastern Europe again and again, hearing conversations, seeing expressions on faces where I had brought Bibles, feeling once more the warmth of spontaneous smiles and fervent embraces, remembering the tragic circumstances I had seen, many of which now haunted me in my helplessness.

I remembered the confession a young woman in Russia had made to me. "My mother died two years ago. Of course I was very sad and cried. But at the same time I experienced something terrible. Deep inside I was really glad. I tried to resist the feeling, but I couldn't get rid of it. Do you know why? Because she had owned a Bible, and now I could get it! All my life I had wanted a Bible of my own. I was seventeen then, and my brother was fifteen. Our father had died in prison many years before.

"But my brother insisted that because he was the son, he should have the Bible. I argued that I was the eldest, and therefore I should get it. I told him he could have everything else—the only thing I wanted was the Bible. We had a bitter quarrel and I felt so ashamed. The Lord spoke to my heart, and I apologized to my brother. The Lord really broke us. We both repented and were reconciled."

As these memories fanned the flame of an increasing desire to help such people, I began to realize that the doctors had never given me a meaningful analysis of my condition. Thinking back, it seemed to me that they had always avoided my questions.

"I think you've been evasive with me," I said to my doctor one day, determined to learn the truth at last. "What are the hopes for my recovery?"

"I think we should wait to discuss that until you're a little stronger. . . ."

"I'm strong enough to know the truth!"

He hesitated, indecision written on his face. "Are you *sure* you don't want to wait a little longer?"

"Just tell me the truth—*now*. I'm a Christian. I can take it. I'm ready to accept whatever is God's will."

"Perhaps you're right," he said with a sigh. "Let's begin by explaining your condition. The paralysis of your right side is due to the destruction of the brain cells controlling that part of the body."

"What do you mean, 'destruction'?"

"Those cells had no blood, no oxygen, for days. When the circulation was finally restored, it was too late. Those cells are dead."

"How can you be sure of this?" I was trying to tell myself that he was wrong. Doctors don't know everything.

"We've verified it a number of ways. One is by the brain

scans we've done—several of them. There's no question about it."

It was more than I could bear to see the pity in his eyes. I turned my face toward the window and tried to concentrate on the clouds of a rain squall moving rapidly toward us. Slowly the implications of what he had said began to sink in. There was more that I should ask, but now I was afraid to. And I'd said I wasn't afraid. The silence was stretching out like a rubber band that had to break.

Forcing myself to face him again, I heard my voice somewhere in the distance asking in a lifeless, fearful tone, a question that I no longer wanted to hear answered. "What does that mean—the cells are dead?"

"The brain is a unique part of the body. Cut your liver in half and it builds itself up again. Cut some skin off a finger, and it grows back. But your brain can't do that. When brain cells die, there's no way to replace them."

"You mean...?"

He nodded. "I'm sorry. You may improve slightly over the next few months, but basically this is it. You'll never recover the use of your right side again!"

I saw the future flash in front of my eyes. Ninna and the children doing everything for me, a paralyzed, helpless invalid—for life! And the work of the mission—finished!

It was as though a nightmare had come true. Just as well to be paralyzed on both sides, for all the good I could do. With absolute finality, in one swift moment, my dreams, my longings, my reasons for living had all been smashed, trampled, ground into the dust. I had wanted to fight a spiritual battle—but I was a broken toy soldier, dropped into a corner to rust.

A loud groaning cry of agony rose from deep within me. Twice I caught it in my throat and choked it back. Then I could hold the bursting dam no longer. Through a blur of tears I saw the indistinct figure of the doctor turn to leave. I buried my face in the pillow. The bed shook as I cried like a child.

In jeering mockery the words echoed hollowly through the empty loneliness of my soul: "I'm strong enough— tell me the truth *now*. I'm a Christian. I can take it."

Now I knew the truth—that I was not strong at all, but the weakest of the weak.

In my despair, I didn't know that I had stumbled upon a rare treasure, one of the great discoveries of my life. Until I knew that, I couldn't know how strong God is.

14

Disaster on a Fool's Mission

The next few days were a torment of mingled night-mare and drug-induced euphoria, the one blurring into the other with nothing sensible in between. Nurses hovered around my bed, taking my temperature and pulse and administering shots and pills to calm my wildly gyrating nerves. In my moments of lucidity, I knew why the doctors had been reluctant to tell me the truth. I could feel myself coming apart, losing control. I found myself afraid to face Ninna, wondering if she knew, and sure she did.

Then slowly, out of the dark tunnel of my despair, I began to realize the mistake that I had made. I had put my hope in doctors and medicine instead of in God. *They* were helpless to replace dead brain cells—but Christ had conquered death. I was grateful for what physicians and nurses had done. To neglect available medical skill would be to tempt God, but my case was beyond the capabilities of medical science. Strangely, when that was settled in my mind, I felt a great sense of relief. There was no doubt now that I qualified for the help that only God could give—and I knew He would not turn me away.

Soon I was up in the wheelchair again, pushing myself around with my left hand, smiling when Ninna came to see me, and telling her that one day I would walk—in God's time. I found myself resting at night and relaxing during the day without the drugs, because now I was resting my case in God's hands. As I did that, the assurance grew within me that I would not only walk, but I would be completely healed and would travel into Eastern Europe once again.

Although naturally right-handed, I was acquiring an amazing dexterity with my left. Gradually I learned to dress myself completely, and to the delight of the nurses, I could now tie my shoes with one hand. Then one day, struck by a sudden inspiration, I begged the therapist to get me an electric typewriter. Perhaps the force of long habit would trigger a reflex action. The next morning when they brought me to the therapy room, it was waiting for me. Wheeling me in front of it, they suspended my right hand from the wrist so that it was hanging in the air, the fingers just touching the keys.

The nurse turned it on, and I began to type, copying the words in a book beside me. The only letters hitting the page were from the keys on the left side of the typewriter. But I persisted, trying to get the mental image of both hands typing automatically. Suddenly there was a twitch from one of my fingers on the right hand . . . then another . . . and another. Three fingers were moving slightly now, not enough to activate the keys, but they were moving.

"I've got something exciting to tell you!" I exclaimed to Ninna that afternoon the moment she stepped inside my room. "I can move three fingers! I almost typed today!"

We both began to cry. She kissed me and squeezed my hand. "I *know* God's going to heal you!" she whispered. "I *know* it!"

I was sure that was the start of something wonderful

that would confound the doctors, but no matter how hard I worked at the typewriter day after day, my three fingers never got beyond that slight movement. Days dragged wearily on. I had been in the hospital three months now. The doctors decided to transfer me to a special therapy hospital with the latest equipment.

There I was trained to stand unassisted, and finally even to walk with a cane. I couldn't move my right leg, but they taught me how to lean on the cane in order to take a short step with my left leg. Then, leaning again and pulling my leg with my back, I could drag my right foot up under me, ready for another short step. My right arm and hand were still useless, but at least I could walk short distances, though haltingly. The doctors decided that further hospitalization and therapy would be of no value. I had reached the peak level of recovery. My discharge papers from the hospital included a doctor's certificate classifying me as totally disabled. That meant the state would continue supporting me and my family as it had been doing for the past four months.

I had never taken a salary from the mission, and the church had stopped my salary after three months in the hospital. I couldn't blame them for that. The church board had voted to replace me. They needed an assistant pastor who didn't always have visions of running off to some Communist country, or touring around Denmark raising funds for a faraway underground church. Anyway, they knew I would never recover.

It wasn't easy coming back to the church, with its memories, in a wheelchair. At first Ninna wheeled me in after the service had started. We stayed at the back near the door, and she took me out during the last hymn, to spare me the strain of facing people and hearing their expressions of sympathy. But gradually I got over that, and it was good to have friends tell me they were praying.

Best of all was just being home after seven months in three hospitals. The children were so glad, and so helpful.

I could read the Bible to them, and pray with them, and even play catch using my left hand. They tried to tie their shoes like I could, and gave up. That small superiority left me still a hero in their eyes.

Sitting at my desk reading the mail and dictating letters, my heart burned more than ever for the work of the mission. I was now in the process of taking it out of the church to set it up under a separate board. I had plenty of time for praying.

I'd been home for a month and was on my knees in prayer one morning when I had the impression that Sonya was in trouble and needed to get out of Bulgaria. I felt a sudden overpowering concern for her, and began to pray earnestly that God would supply her need, whatever it was. That was when the Lord seemed to say something very strange. I was to be the one to bring her out. It made no sense at all!

"While I was praying early this morning," I said to Ninna at breakfast two hours later, "I had a strong feeling that Sonya's in trouble and needs to escape to the West."

"You haven't heard from her for a long time, have you?" said Ninna thoughtfully.

I shook my head. "What I don't understand. . . well, maybe I shouldn't tell you. . . but it seemed to me that the Lord was saying that I'm supposed to go and bring her out!"

With the excitement of getting the children fed and off to school, we forgot all about Sonya. About an hour after breakfast, I was trying to dictate some letters when the phone rang. It was long distance. I immediately recognized the voice of the director of another Scandinavian mission working behind the Iron Curtain.

After a brief exchange of greetings, he said, "We've just received an urgent message for you from Sonya." Suddenly I was pressing the receiver hard against my ear, hanging onto every word, light-headed with excitement.

"Sonya and her brother and his wife have been called

in for questioning by the secret police several times in the last few days. They're being followed everywhere they go, and expect to be arrested at any moment. Her brother has those three small children, you know, and they can't run the risk of going to prison and having those innocent kids put into an atheistic boarding home. They want to escape, and they think you're supposed to help them!"

My head was swimming. "They want *me* to help?"

"They're going to try to get to Kranos' house in Hungary. They want you to meet them there with a car, and take them into Austria."

"Do they have passports?"

"That's all fixed. You know."

I should have understood what he meant, but didn't want to spell it out on the phone: that I was to borrow passports from Danish friends who looked like them. But my mind had gone blank. The only thing I could think of was that God was trying to tell me something that I was afraid to hear.

"You know I just got out of the hospital, brother. My right side is useless. In my condition..."

"I can understand that. I'm only passing along the message. Why don't you pray about it and let me know— but right away. If you can't do it, I'll have to get someone else."

"I'll pray about it," I said weakly, "and let you know."

I let the receiver fall back onto its cradle with a clatter, and leaned back in my wheelchair. I was trembling.

"Hans! Who was it?" Ninna was standing in the doorway of my study. I pulled myself together.

"It was about Sonya. She and her brother's family have to escape. They're in trouble with the police and want me..." I hesitated, then rephrased what I was going to say. "They must not have heard about my condition yet, because they want me to bring a car and take them out."

"How could you get them over the border? Do they have passports?"

"I think so—but look at *me*! I'd just be a burden. If only I were well. . . ."

Neither of us spoke for several minutes. I didn't want to go. But I didn't want to admit it. There was one way to get out of it graciously. I'd leave it up to Ninna. She wouldn't want me to go, and for *her* sake I'd have to refuse.

I broke the uncomfortable silence. "What do *you* think?"

Ninna's answer was immediate. "But, Hans, of course you should go! Didn't the Lord already tell you that early this morning?"

"He told me Sonya was in trouble. . . but I'm not sure He told me I was to go. . . ."

"Hans, you told me at breakfast that the Lord said you were the one to go." She put her hand on my shoulder. "I know it will be awfully hard—driving, and getting in and out of the car, the plane—but if God wants you to go, then He'll give you the strength!"

I felt trapped and ashamed. "I said I'd pray about it. Let me ask the Lord again."

For three hours I wrestled with the Lord, not asking His will, but telling Him mine. If only I were well, but He hadn't healed me yet—I reminded Him of that reproachfully. It was unreasonable to expect a paralytic to do something like this! But the more I prayed, the more I knew that God was not going to give in to my whining. I *had* to go, and He promised to bring me through. I would bring the refugees safely into Austria.

Arriving in Vienna, I rented a Volkswagen bus at the airport and drove to the Scandinavian Airlines office in town. Before leaving Copenhagen, I had sent a telegram to Brother Kranos. It read: "Call Vienna [I gave the SAS office number] between 15:00 and 16:00 today—Hans." Waiting in the Vienna office, my apprehension grew as the hands of the clock moved past 3:30, 3:45, 4:00. About two minutes after 4:00 I was called to the phone.

"Hans! Is that you? Your telegram didn't say what city to call!"

"But I put Vienna in the telegram!"

"There was just a number, but no city. We prayed, and just a few minutes ago the Lord told us you were in Vienna!"

"Okay," I said, suddenly remembering we were probably being listened to. "I'll be in Kapuvar tomorrow. Why don't you take the train down there? I'll meet you at the station. It would be great to see you!"

Arriving at Kapuvar shortly after noon, I learned that there were three trains a day coming from Kranos' town. I would have to meet each one. It wasn't easy for a man in my condition to shuttle back and forth from the hotel to the station and to get in and out of the car, but I had to meet each train they might be on. By the second day, with no sign of them, my growing dismay had turned to alarm. What could be keeping them? Had they misunderstood me and gone to the wrong town? Or worse—had they been traced to Kranos' house and arrested?

Then at last there they were, stepping off a train, running toward me. We embraced exuberantly on the platform. I felt giddy with the sudden intensity of our meeting, the unrealness of being there and seeing them, the uncertainty of what lay ahead.

"Hans! Your leg!" Sonya whispered sympathetically, looking me up and down in pity. "The arm, too?"

There was no time for that. "Where's your baggage?" I asked.

Georgi, Sonya's brother, held up one small suitcase and shrugged. That was it for the six of them. He could understand a little German, but like his wife and the three children, spoke only Bulgarian.

We moved toward the car, slowly for my sake. Sonya sat in front so we could talk and she could give me directions from the map. Georgi sat in the middle seat with the eldest child, and Tanya, his wife, was in back with the other two.

"How did you manage to get the passports?" I asked Sonya when we had settled into our seats.

"What passports?" she replied, looking mystified. "Weren't you going to bring some?"

I was stunned. "You have none? How did you get into Hungary?"

"Our identity papers got us from one Communist country into another, but we can't get out to the West. We thought you were bringing passports!"

Sonya began to talk rapidly to the others in Bulgarian. Then silence filled the car. I felt ill. Clutching the steering wheel with my one good hand until my knuckles turned white, I tried to quell the panic exploding inside me.

"It's my fault," I said at last. "I misunderstood."

"Don't blame yourself," said Sonya generously. "We're in the Lord's hands. If He allowed it, then we know there must be a reason."

Feeling a sudden inspiration, I asked Sonya to spread the map out in front of us. "Perhaps at a small border station..." I began, thinking out loud. "I'm trying to remember...someone told me of a place...there's only one guard on each side. There! That's it. Guide me to that one!"

Zigzagging our way up a narrow road into the mountains, we came in about two hours to an isolated border crossing. It was just the way it had been described—a small shelter hut and barrier on each side, with only one guard for each country. Stopping in front of the barricade, I climbed out of the car as quickly as I could and hurried to meet the Hungarian guard just coming out of his shelter. I hoped to keep him as far from the car as I could in order to minimize the presence of the others.

"But you're Danish," he said as soon as he had opened my passport. "You can't cross the border here. This road is only for Austrian citizens." He handed back the passport.

I had brought plenty of cash and extricated a hundred-dollar bill from among several others, doing it inside my pocket so he wouldn't see how much I had. I pressed it into his hand. "My friends and I have to be in Vienna in a few hours," I said persuasively. "These regulations aren't intended to work a hardship. You could let us through as a favor.... Okay?"

He nodded almost imperceptibly, glancing out of the corner of his eye in the direction of the Austrian guard. The latter had been watching from his side of the border about fifty feet away, and was now walking slowly toward us. I congratulated myself. This was going to be easier than I had thought.

"What's going on here?" demanded the Austrian as he came up. "Let me see your passports!"

I handed mine to him. "Please!" I begged. "We're not Austrians, but we have to get to Vienna in..."

He was already closing the passport and handing it back to me. "You can't pass here!" he said with finality. "Now turn around and go back to a proper crossing!"

I had another hundred-dollar bill ready and held it out toward him. "We have an Austrian car. There's no need to be more technical than that."

He shook his head, averting his gaze from the money. "But we're late!" I said. "What if we miss our plane?" Moving closer so the Hungarian couldn't hear me, I whispered, "How much?"

His jaw hardened and he drew himself up stiffly, a look of utter disdain on his face. "Are you crazy!" He spat the words out. Turning on his heel, he stalked back to his side of the border, where he leaned against the barricade, lit a cigarette, and watched.

Flushed with embarrassment and anger, I turned back to the Communist guard. "He's very particular, that chap," I said indignantly, waving a thumb in the direction of the Austrian. "And very inhuman. He insists that we go a hundred miles out of our way!"

I shook my head in disgust and held out my hand. He gave me back the hundred-dollar bill. Shrugging his shoulders, he lit a cigarette and watched as I climbed back into the car.

"We almost made it!" I said to Sonya as I turned around and headed back down the mountain. "I think I've got the right idea. Find another small road on the map that crosses the border and we'll try that one. Maybe the Austrian guard there won't be such a stickler for technicalities."

By the time we had descended into a long, narrow valley, a heavy rain had begun to fall. Following the map, Sonya directed me to turn left at a fork at the head of the valley, and we soon found ourselves climbing steeply into the mountains again. As we drove higher, the rain became so heavy that I could hardly see. Lightning flashed above us and thunder reverberated in the steep canyon to our left. The defroster wasn't working and the windows began to fog badly. Sonya found a rag under the seat and periodically wiped the windshield in front of me. Suddenly the pavement ended. The already-narrow road became a sea of mud laced with crisscrossing rivulets.

Certain now that we must be on the wrong road, I was peering through the rain for a place to turn around when the tires began to slip, causing the car to fishtail crazily. Before I knew what was happening, the rear of the vehicle swung around and off the side of the road into a small ditch that was fast becoming a creek. I tried to back out, but now the accelerator had stuck at full throttle, and the rear wheels spun as though they were suspended in air. Turning off the racing engine, I started to open the door. Sonya grabbed my arm.

"Look!" she gasped.

Then I saw them, too—more than a dozen soldiers, each carrying an automatic rifle. We were surrounded!

Through the fogged windows I could see that every weapon was pointed at us. And the noise! They were yelling like excited children, as though they had just captured a carload of enemy spies.

The door on my side of the car was wrenched open, and I found myself staring into the excited face of a young officer who was apparently in charge of the platoon. The drawn revolver in his hand was aimed at my chest, and he was shouting at me in Hungarian.

"He's ordering you out," said Sonya, "but our identity papers! You've got them! They'll search you!"

While sliding sideways through the open door, I managed to pull the refugees' papers from my coat pocket and leave them on the seat behind me. I sensed more than saw Sonya wrap them quickly in the rag she was holding, and begin diligently to wipe the moisture from the inside of the windshield.

I hadn't thought to grab my cane, and now had to hang on for support to the handle of the door I had closed behind me. I felt myself settling into mud over the tops of my shoes. Even with the cane I would be helpless in this. The officer had come around behind me and jabbed his gun into my back. Instinctively I raised my good left hand over my head. Unable now to hold onto the car for support, I swayed precariously on the edge of the ditch.

I couldn't understand a word of Hungarian, but the officer was waving with one hand toward the top of a hill that I could dimly see rising steeply in front of me through the mist and rain. He was shoving at my back with the point of his gun, and I knew that I was being commanded to go up the hill. But I was helpless to move even an inch.

When I failed to budge, the order was repeated, this time louder and more insistently and accompanied by another shove from the revolver that nearly knocked me to the ground. Somehow I kept my feet, knowing that a sudden move to grab the door handle would draw a shot.

Instinctively I knew that orders are usually given three times and no more, but beyond that dread anticipation my mind refused to look. Out of the corner of my eye I could see that several soldiers had opened the doors on the other side of the car and were searching through it.

I stood mesmerized by the flashing lightning, rolling thunder, pounding rain, and shouting men. My mind seemed as immobile as my paralyzed right side. I didn't think to pray. I couldn't think at all. Numbly I had the vague realization that this young officer was so excited at having made his first catch that it would be impossible to change his mind even if I spoke his language.

For the third and, I was sure, last time, he ordered me to move forward. I felt the sharp pain of the gun barrel as it was jabbed forcefully into the small of my back. On the verge of losing my balance from the force of the thrust and helpless to respond to his final command, I awaited the bullet.

15
Not My Will, but Thine

An ear-shattering roar filled the air. For a split second I wondered that I felt no pain. Then, as the thunder passed overhead to echo down the valley, I was suddenly jolted by what seemed to be a massive charge of electricity shooting through my right side. It was like an explosion of life itself, bringing instant strength to every nerve and fiber. To my utter astonishment, I realized that I was now walking!

A few more moments, and I found myself climbing a hill so steep that at times we had to use our hands to clutch at rocks and bushes, clawing our way up the rough and slippery terrain. Scrambling ahead of the young officer, I was amazed to find that my right leg was as strong as the left, and my right arm was swinging free, pushing branches aside, pulling me up over rocks. But I had little time to savor the wonder of instant healing. The heavy breathing of the grimly determined soldier on my heels, grunting an occasional oath as he slipped on mud or rock, and the fear of what lay ahead, for me and the refugees, drove every other thought from my mind.

On top of the short rise, we pushed our way through

a tight clump of firs and came to a sheltered clearing dominated by a sprawling log cabin. Waving me inside with his gun, my captor slammed the door shut on the storm behind us and presented me to a higher ranking officer, whom I took to be in charge of the area. He was sitting at a desk poring over some maps. After a brief discussion between the two of them in Hungarian, the commandant asked, in German, for my identity papers. Handing my passport to him, I hastened to explain.

"I'm a tourist," I said apologetically. "We were on our way to Vienna and got lost. I didn't know that was military territory. . . ."

Giving me a skeptical look, he began to go carefully through my passport. When he came to the stamp indicating the border crossing where I had entered Hungary, he stroked his chin thoughtfully and gave me another penetrating look.

"I see what you've done," he said gruffly, handing back my passport. "Look here." He turned one of the maps on his desk around so I could see it and traced the point of a pencil along a line that appeared to be the small road we had taken. "See this fork back here? You should have gone to the right. That would have taken you back to the border where you entered. Instead, you turned left. Go back down to the fork, make a sharp left and another left at the main road. You can't miss it."

"Thank you very much, sir," I said, feeling more grateful than he could have imagined. "I'm sorry for all the trouble, but I have another problem. Our car is stuck in a ditch. We can't turn it around."

He spoke rapidly to the younger officer, who only now, and I thought rather reluctantly, put his gun back into the holster.

"Okay," said the commandant after their brief discussion. "He has enough men down there. They'll pull you out. And be careful about wrong turns after this!"

"Hans! You're healed!" exclaimed Sonya as soon as the

car had been pulled from the ditch and we had started back down the narrow road, throttle still stuck and engine roaring at full speed as I worked the clutch in and out. "Praise God! The Lord is with us!"

I told her briefly what had happened at the command post, and she related how she had continued wiping the windows with the rag that hid their identity papers, while three soldiers searched the car, demanding passports. Sonya had pretended not to understand, and in spite of the noise of thunder, rain, and wind, and yelling soldiers, the children had miraculously remained asleep. If they had awakened and cried out in Bulgarian, our arrest would have been immediate.

"What are we going to do now?" asked Sonya anxiously after we had regained the main road.

"It's all my fault," I confessed bitterly. "I haven't been asking God what to do, but I've been trying to scheme and bribe our way across the border and I almost got us all arrested. I'm sorry."

"But the Lord was faithful, wasn't He!"

"Yes, in spite of me," I admitted soberly. "Now we must get some sleep. I know a pastor in a town about eighty kilometers from here. I'm sure he'll take us in for the night."

It was after 11:00 P.M. when we arrived. There was still a narrow finger of light visible under a blind. Leaving the others in the car, I knocked at the front door. I heard hesitant footsteps and a voice called softly through the door.

"Who is it?"

"Hans Kristian!" I whispered back.

There was the sound of a latch and chain being withdrawn, and the door was flung open. "Hans!" the pastor exclaimed. "What brings you here at this time of the night?"

"I have six people with me," I said, purposely omitting any information that could become a burden if he were

questioned later. "It could be dangerous for you, but we
need some sleep badly. They haven't had any for nearly
two days."

"Come in," he said simply. I turned and motioned to
the others waiting in the car.

"Look at your suit!" exclaimed his wife when we were
all in the house and the pastor was bustling around for
chairs. "You're soaked to the skin! Jon, get him wrapped
in a bathrobe and a blanket and give me those clothes
so I can dry them."

After a hot drink, the exhausted refugees, wrapped in
quilts, fell asleep on the floor. I stepped through a side
door into the tiny church adjoining the house. Groping
in the darkness, I found a wooden bench in the back and
fell on my knees in front of it. Shivering from the cold,
I pulled the blanket closer around me and began to pray.
There was a secret I couldn't share with Sonya.

"You know my heart, Lord. You know I don't want to
be here. I can admit it to You, but I'm ashamed to tell
anyone else. It's not my love for these refugees that
brought me here. It's not even my love for You, or obedience either. I was afraid of what Ninna—and others—
would think if I didn't come. I was afraid to be exposed
as a hypocrite. And now I'm afraid to try to cross the
border again. Oh, God! What can I do?"

As I knelt there in shame, it seemed that the rottenness
of my heart lay exposed before me. I had tried to excuse
myself because I was paralyzed, and God had healed me.
Now I was more afraid than ever. If only there were a way
to do it, I would leave the refugees to their fate. But I was
trapped, afraid to try the border again for fear of arrest,
and afraid not to try because of what people would say.

And my healing—such an incredible thing! I tried to
thank God for that, but my burden was too great. "Thank
You, Lord," I began. "What a miracle! Help me to be more
grateful. I'm ashamed to admit it, but it almost seems as
nothing to be healed and left in this predicament. How

can we cross the border without passports!"

My thoughts went back to the night I had first met Sonya. God had told her to take a different way to church and to look for two men from the West on the street. She had found us and guided us. Her life had been an inspiration. God had so often spoken to her and protected her. Why didn't He do it now? I felt resentful. Why wasn't she on her knees in prayer, carrying her own burdens, instead of sleeping soundly in the house next door? Why was I left to carry the load alone?

Slowly I realized what was wrong. I was still trying to act strong, even though I knew I was so weak. God couldn't do anything until I quit trying to be the big hero, the great rescuer of refugees. Sonya had done so much for me, and I had determined to show her that I could do something, too. It had been "I...I...I...." *I* had a clever plan. *I* had schemed to get us across *my* way. *I* had even tried to bribe. And God had been in none of it. *I* had been too busy with my own plans to ask Him to reveal *His*. In the quiet darkness it was plain to me now.

"Lord, I'm sorry," I cried. "I didn't seek Your will—I asked You to bless *my* plans. Mercifully, You even did that. You provided a way of escape when I got us in trouble. You even healed me. Oh, God! How often do I have to learn the same lesson! Not another step now until You show me the way!"

Turning from myself and my problems toward the Lord, I could see that there was so much to thank Him for, and my heart began to fill with gratitude and praise. Not just for the events of this one night—my healing, keeping the children asleep, rescuing us from the soldiers—but I looked back over my life and saw how remarkably God had guided and blessed, how much He had done in His grace. How my fears and unbelief now must grieve His heart! He was able to get us across into Austria. Of course it was impossible for me. But the things that are impossible with men are possible with God. All we had to do was to let Him show us the way.

Now I was listening, waiting to hear His voice. At about 1:00 A.M. He spoke to me. Not audibly, but with an inner assurance and confidence so deep and strong that I could only obey. At exactly 3:00 A.M. we were to cross the border at the same point where I had entered three days before. It was a large, well-lighted and heavily traveled crossing with many guards, but this time God would take us across, and we had nothing to fear.

I lay down on the floor wrapped in the blanket and fell instantly asleep. At 2:00 A.M. I awakened and hurried back into the house.

"It's time to get up," I called.

Someone turned on a light. "It's only 2:00!" exclaimed Sonya. "We've scarcely been asleep!"

I whispered to her so the pastor and his wife wouldn't hear. "The Lord has spoken to me. We must be at the border at 3:00 A.M. He will take us across." She explained to her brother and sister-in-law. After a quick cup of hot coffee, the pastor prayed that God would keep us safe, and we said a hasty good-bye. When I turned the car onto the main Budapest-Vienna highway two kilometers from the village, my watch stood at 2:30 A.M.

"We must pray," I said to Sonya. I began. "Lord, in faith trusting Your promise, we ask You to blind the eyes of the guards at the border. Don't let them see anyone in this car but me. Cover my friends with Your hand!"

Sonya interpreted, and then we all continued together to ask this miracle from the Lord, they in Bulgarian and I in Danish. Everyone prayed loudly at once, not listening to each other nor trying to impress one another with fine words, but communing with God from our hearts.

As we prayed, I felt the presence and power of God come into the car. Our prayers turned to joyful praise. Every fear had gone, and we began to thank Him for what we *knew* He was going to do.

It was exactly 3:00 A.M. when we arrived at the border.

The station was flooded with light. I turned off the racing engine several hundred yards away and tried to coast in quietly. Two guards were searching a car. I pulled in behind it, and another uniformed man came out of the building.

Rolling down my window, I reached through and handed him my passport without saying a word. He examined it carefully, looked at the picture and then at me to be sure I was the same person. Then he pressed his face against the window just behind me and glanced through the interior of the car. I had no suitcase, just a toothbrush in my pocket because, in my paralyzed state, I couldn't carry any luggage. The one small suitcase the refugees had brought was sitting beside Sonya's brother on the middle seat. The guard's eyes settled on that.

"Let me see your suitcase," he said in German.

Climbing out from behind the wheel, I walked around and pulled open the side door, reached in and opened the suitcase for him. He stuck his head inside the car, almost touching Georgi, and felt through the suitcase carefully. Closing it, he glanced once more through the car and straightened up with a satisfied grunt.

"Have a nice trip," he said, and handing back my passport motioned me to proceed. I walked around and climbed into the driver's seat again. I waved at him as the engine started and we pulled away.

"Praise God!" I exclaimed. "At least we're past them...and now we only have to face the Austrians!"

"What if they stop us?" asked Sonya. "They wouldn't send us back, would they?"

"I don't think they would, if you ask for asylum. But they would probably have to arrest all of us."

The Austrian border station was about two hundred yards ahead of us. With the gas pedal still stuck at full throttle, I was holding the clutch in halfway to keep down the speed. The roar of the racing engine gave a rude and embarrassing announcement calling attention to our approach. A large truck was parked at the border, and all the customs officials were busily occupied closely examining its cargo. As we approached with an unnerving roar, an official looked up with a startled expression, seemed to hesitate for a moment, then waved to me to go around the truck and continue on.

The refugees were talking excitedly to one another now. I was praising God in my heart and concentrating on the road.

"Do you know what we're saying?" asked Sonya.

I could imagine a lot of things. I smiled and shook my head.

"We've been telling one another that we feel like the children of Israel when the waters of Jordan separated and they walked through into the Promised Land!"

A few more kilometers and I stopped the car. Everyone jumped out. We fell on our knees in the wet grass beside the road. Oblivious of the rain that was still falling, we raised our tear-stained faces and thanked our heavenly Father.

16

Back to Russia

Arriving at Copenhagen's airport a different man in many ways than when I had left, my first impulse was to phone Ninna and tell her everything. Instead, I took a taxi home to surprise her. I wanted her to see for herself before I said anything. My heart was pounding as I fitted the key into the door of our apartment and turned the lock quietly. Stepping into the entry hall, I heard the warm sounds of lively conversation coming from the living room to my right. I recognized the voices of Rene and his wife, Ruth. That was a pleasant surprise. How appropriate that they should be there!

With fingers trembling from excitement, I clutched the knob, turned it gently, and opened the door into the living room. Taking a few steps, I stood just inside the room regarding the three of them with a smile. They were so busy talking that they hardly noticed me.

"Oh, there you are!" exclaimed Ninna, interrupting what Rene was saying at the moment. "I was expecting you to phone."

"How are Sonya and her brother and his family?" asked Rene. "Are they...?"

"Thanks be to God," I replied, "they're all safe in Austria!"

"Praise the Lord!" the three of them exclaimed in unison.

Ninna had been looking at me closely. "Hans, you look horrible! You need a shave—and your suit! It's so filthy!"

I was watching them with an amused smile. "Do you notice anything else?"

"No, but tell us about your trip."

I took a few steps forward, swinging my right arm and lifting my right leg. "Do you see something now?"

Ninna gasped and put both hands to her face. I ran to her and held her in my arms. She clung to me, crying softly. "Thank God! Thank God...!" she said quietly over and over.

Next I hugged Rene and Ruth. By now the children had come running in to see what was happening, and they began to hug me, too, shouting, "God healed Daddy! Daddy's been healed!"

When the emotion subsided, I sat down and told about my trip, especially about the spiritual lessons I had learned. But I asked them not to say anything about the escape of the refugees until they were safely in Sweden.

The next day I drove to the hospital to present myself for an examination. The doctors were amazed when they saw me. I didn't want the state to be supporting me anymore since I was no longer disabled, and tried to convince them to certify that I was now in good health.

"We can't find anything wrong with you," said the doctor who had the authority to remove me from disability status. "But this is impossible. We can't accept 'healing miracles,' I'm responsible for you. It may be just a temporary reversal, and you'll be back where you were. I can't certify that you're well."

I tried to argue, but he was adamant and told me to come back in a month for another examination. Six months went by—months of vigor and long hours working for the mission—and finally I determined not to take *no* as an answer from the doctors any longer. It was not right to call me "disabled" and to have the state pay my support just because medical science had no explanation for miracles.

"You have to sign me off of this foolish disability," I insisted, after they had given me another complete physical. The doctor went through the usual questions again: Did I have pain in my right side, the arm or leg; did I have headaches; could I sleep at night without any pills; how long had I been off all medication; did I get easily fatigued? I gave him my usual answers. We had been through this many times, and all the doctors ever said was, "Impossible!"

"I know God healed me," I persisted. "I've told you how it happened. Your problem is you're trying to understand it in medical terms. You don't have to understand it—just believe it."

Stubbornly the doctor shook his head. "I still don't believe in miracles. And I don't have to believe. I can see for myself that there's nothing wrong with you. That takes no faith. I have no explanation to put on my report, but I'll change your status to 'physically fit.' "

The mission had a new board now, independent from any church. I was training new couriers, teaching them how to memorize names and addresses, how to use codes, how to exercise prudence in any contacts with Christians in order to avoid unnecessary trouble for them. They were cautioned to avoid political discussions except with unbelievers and then only when necessary. They were reminded of the difference between the Bible, which is the Christian's handbook, and all other religious books. No valid complaint could be made for bringing Bibles across borders, but any other book, no matter how biblical, could be labeled "propaganda" and even interpreted as being political indoctrination.

But the most important lesson I tried to teach was the

necessity of keeping in touch with God—of hearing His voice and being motivated by His love and surrendered to His will. This had been one of the greatest and most difficult lessons of my life.

The First Commandment, so I had always thought, was to love God with all my heart. Only when I read more carefully did I see that Christ had said: This is the first and great commandment, *"Hear, O Israel. . . and* thou shalt love the Lord thy God." That was when I began to grasp more fully the secret of the Christianity I had seen behind the Iron Curtain. So many of those believers were really in touch with God. I had always been so busy trying to serve God and calling out to Him in prayer that I hadn't really listened to Him speak to me. Finally I was beginning to learn that.

Jesus had said: My sheep hear My voice and they follow Me. I had to listen for His voice, for His Commandments, for His promises to my heart. It was one thing to read and even memorize the Bible—and another thing entirely to take it as my own, to hear God speak to *me* through His Word. I must hear Him tell me what to do in life, step-by-step, and let Him guide me in each situation I faced.

One day as I prayed and listened, it seemed to me that God was saying, "I want you to go back to Russia again." I had been told officially that I was never to return, but that was the word of men. Now God was saying something else, and I wanted to obey. First, I would see how Ninna felt. We were in life together.

"I don't see any problem," she said. "They told you never to come back, so I doubt that they'll give you a visa. But if they do, we'll know it's God's will."

The visa was granted, and this time I went by plane with a group. In Moscow, like good tourists, my traveling companion and I visited Lenin's tomb. More respect is demanded in that mausoleum than most Christians show in their churches. One need only observe the extreme reverence, the look of worship in the eyes of the Russian people viewing the lifelike, waxed, and cosmetically prepared remains of Lenin displayed in its glass vault, to realize that even atheists have a religion. This is their cathedral, and Lenin is their god.

A Moscow newspaper published the confession of a bus driver who admitted that he had driven past a scheduled stop. A schoolgirl waiting to get the bus had reported him. In his confession, he admitted that his greatest crime had been to forget to ask himself what Lenin would have done in that situation. He vowed to make this the rule of his life ever after—to do only what Lenin would do!

One of my objectives on this trip was to visit the Historic Museum of Atheism and Religion in Leningrad. "We'd like to have a guide this afternoon at 2:00," I said to a young woman behind an Intourist desk in the lobby of our hotel.

"That's fine. What language do you prefer?"

"Danish, German, English—it doesn't matter."

"Oh, that makes it very easy," she said with a smile. "We'll have a guide for you right here at 2:00. Now, where would you like to go?"

"We want to visit the Historic Museum of Atheism and Religion."

She looked suddenly embarrassed and coughed uncomfortably. "Oh, we can't do that!" she exclaimed, glancing around nervously.

"Why not?" I demanded.

"I'm sorry, but I made a mistake. All of our guides are engaged."

I went to another part of the hotel where there was also a representative from Intourist. "I'd like a guide for this afternoon at 2:00," I said. "English, Danish or German."

"That's easy," said the girl. "We have lots of guides. Let me put your name down. Where did you want to go?"

"To the Historic Museum of Atheism and Religion."

Again that embarrassed expression. "Well, I'm sorry, but we don't have any guides after all."

"Yes, you do have guides," I insisted. "I *know* you have!"

"But it would be very expensive—eight rubles!"

"That's fine."

"But we really have none for the Museum of Atheism. The only guides we have for that are for the Russian people. They don't speak other languages."

I continued to insist, as one must in Russia, and finally we got our guide. She was a tiny girl from North Korea (the picture of sweetness and politeness). She was studying in Leningrad, and spoke fluent English and Russian.

The museum is located in what used to be one of the largest and most beautiful cathedrals in Leningrad. When we entered, one of the first things that caught my eye was a picture of Yuri Gagarin.

"What does it say under his picture?" I asked.

"Oh, nothing special," replied our guide.

"Of course it does, or it wouldn't be here," I insisted. "Please translate it for us."

"Well, it says he was the first human in space, and he looked all around up there and didn't see God. So we're sure God doesn't exist."

"What else?"

"Nothing else."

"Yes, there is. I can see a lot more writing than that."

"Okay. Then it says in case anyone argues that God is deeper in space than Gagarin went, Soviet scientists have calculated that even if He did exist, He's so far away that it would take thirty million years for prayer to reach Him and thirty million years for the answer to get back. So it tells our people not to waste their time praying."

I burst out laughing. I couldn't help myself. "That's childish!" I exclaimed. "Do you believe that?"

We continued slowly and came to some more pictures. "What are those about?" I asked and went over for a closer look.

She came and stood beside me. "The man sitting at the

desk was once a Christian, but now he's an atheist, and that's why he has a good job. Those men—well, that one is a Baptist, and that's an Adventist, and that one's a Jehovah's Witness. They've broken the law, so they're in prison."

A group of very young schoolchildren came in, apparently accompanied by their teacher. I said to our guide, "Let's follow them, and you interpret for us."

But one of the museum guards, looking very disturbed, came over to remind us that we had to keep our distance from all Russians. He warned us that if we continued to follow so closely, we would be put out.

I had hoped to have the same experience as one of my friends once had in an atheistic museum in the USSR. The first thing in the museum had been a picture of Lenin as a boy. The teacher was saying to her class, "Here children, look! This boy is only twelve years old. See what beautiful eyes he has! And you can tell by his face that he is a good boy. How intelligent he looks! That is Lenin. Here is a picture of his parents. He always obeyed his parents, and he always got the best marks in school. You should try to be just like him! Always do what Lenin would do!"

There was a great deal of fanciful nonsense about evolution in the museum as a supposed proof that the universe happened by chance, and therefore God didn't exist. But there were a number of factual displays that one could not argue against because they told the truth. One was an icon that was obviously genuine. It looked as though it had been kissed and fondled and wept over thousands of times. The "saint" pictured in it supposedly wept when people prayed to it. The display revealed how this deceptive religious trick worked. There was a tiny hole in the corner of each eye from which a tube connected to a bottle of water behind. A priest hiding behind the icon would release some water whenever anyone came to pray and watch the saint "cry." From this evidence, the descriptive writing under the icon concluded that all religion was a fraud.

This argument was pursued in other displays that were just as factual. It was pointed out that the cathedrals in Russia had been built for the wealthy few, and ordinary people were not allowed inside. Large cathedrals were often built by a family of the aristocracy for their own private use. Most of the cathedrals still standing in Russia, especially the famous ones, had numerous small rooms but no large one for public worship.

There were references to the inquisitions; to the fact that at one time there were two popes, each claiming descent from Peter and supremacy over the church; to the wars fought between Catholics and Protestants, each claiming to have the true faith; to the plundering Crusaders, robbing and murdering in the name of Christ. A great deal of emphasis was given also to the way in which religious leaders and churches have so often used their power to keep the common people in ignorance, milking them of their pitiful earnings by pretending that gifts to the church would buy favor with God.

"Many of these things are very true," I admitted to our guide. "However, that's not what Jesus taught, but what in fact He condemned! Anyone who practices such crimes against humanity is not a true Christian."

"But they claim to be Christians," she said.

"There are also people who claim to be Communists," I reminded her, "who do not live up to the high ideals of sharing equally with everyone. Many terrible crimes have been committed by Communists—take Stalin for instance. Does that disprove the high ideals of communism?"

She shook her head.

"No church has ever come close to equaling the crimes of Stalin. I doubt that all of the Crusaders put together committed as much murder and robbery as he. So although this museum tells some truth about the evils men do under the cloak of Christianity, it doesn't make honest conclusions from these facts. Instead, it lies and does its own evil. It's deliberately dishonest to point out the crimes of hypocrites and religious organizations, implying that this is true Christianity. And it's dishonest to hide the well-known fact that there have always been true followers of Christ in this world who have been the leaders in educating and liberating humanity from tyrants."

Our guide listened politely to what I had to say, but it seemed to have little effect upon her. Apparently her indoctrination had been so thorough that she felt it was absurd even to listen to other viewpoints. Or maybe she had seen some religious hypocrisy that had touched her life and turned her away. I wasn't able to find out.

This museum is only a sample of the ingenious ideas of the Ministry of Religion, which has one of the largest budgets in the entire Soviet Union. A staff of about two million full-time workers in the organization Znanie are dedicated to the task of "educating" the Russian people to reject the false teachings of religion. There are about 15,000 such staff members in Moscow alone. Scores of high-quality films promoting atheism and debunking religion are shown throughout Russia and approximately 40,000 lectures are held each day in schools, factories, clubs, and other groups—all "proving" there is no God.

In spite of this assault on religion, more people believe in God in Russia today than ever before in its history. The Ministry of Religion itself has estimated that more than 60 percent of the population believe in God, even after being subjected to the psychological pressures and the barrage of antireligious propaganda that is a way of life for every Soviet citizen from earliest childhood.

Leaving the museum, we crossed the city to meet a friend of Aida Skripnikova, who led us to a secret meeting held in a home on the outskirts of Leningrad. The young man interpreted as I spoke briefly to the group. I had hoped to see Aida there, but she was away at the time.

However, there were other young people there just like her, unknown by name to the world, but known to God. Filled to overflowing with the love of Christ, they were willing to go to prison or to death for Him.

As I left the meeting later that night, one thought was going through my mind: With 40,000 lectures every day and 2,000,000 full-time atheistic propagandists at work, it was a one-sided battle which should have ended in an overwhelming victory, at least in fifty years—yet it hadn't. One needed no stronger evidence to know that materialism could not satisfy man's spirit, and physical weapons such as torture and prison could never win a spiritual battle.

17

Capitalism, Communism, and Christianity

"One thing I'll admit the capitalists are ahead of us in, and that's crime!" Fyodr's deep-set steel gray eyes twinkled. He leaned back and laughed.

"No argument there," I conceded. "You've got me cold. I'm not afraid to walk the streets at night here in Leningrad, but I'd be crazy to try the same thing in Los Angeles or New York or a hundred other American cities."

"No murders, holdups, riots, or rape on our public streets anywhere in Russia!" he boasted. "We don't allow it!" The smug look gave place to a mischievous grin. "But don't divert attention to the Americans. Your own city of Copenhagen is the pornography capital of the world. That seems to be what people love in that *Christian* country."

"Oh, I don't think Christians go for that, and Denmark isn't really a Christian country. There's no such thing," I replied cautiously, deliberately avoiding that opening. I'd have to come back to it later. I didn't want Fyodr to know I was a Christian—yet. "Denmark has gone wild on sex," I admitted. "I appreciate the ban on pornography in the

Soviet Union—and so would most of the people in Denmark."

Fyodr worked for Intourist as an English-speaking guide and had led us on a short tour of Leningrad that afternoon. We had taken a liking to one another, and now after dinner we had been sitting for two hours in the lobby of the hotel engrossed in a discussion of the differences between communism and capitalism. He had a quick mind and a keen sense of humor that I appreciated.

One of the things that had often disappointed me during my travels in Eastern Europe was the fact that I had never been able to engage a real Communist in serious discussion. Strangely enough, dedicated Communists are extremely rare in Communist countries. The revolution was supposed to be for the common man, yet fifty years later 90 percent of the masses are still not members of the party. And most of those who are seem to be in it for the extra benefits that go with membership, rather than from any sincere idealism. At least the ones I had encountered always disappointed me with the shallowness of their reasoning, as though they were parroting Marxist dogma without having thought it through for themselves.

Often I had asked God to lead me to someone truly dedicated to the ideals of communism, one who really believed in them deeply and knew *why* he did. Fyodr was the answer to that prayer. A brilliant student doing graduate work at Moscow University, a dedicated idealist, he was just the person who could explain to me the reasons for his devotion to the Communist faith and with whom I could reason about the kingdom of God. But I was purposely deferring the latter subject until the end of our conversation, knowing that if he suspected I was a Christian, deep prejudices would prevent him from hearing what I said or obligate him to break off our discussion.

"How do you know so much about Denmark?" I asked him. "You've never been there, have you?"

"We have newspapers and books. I've read a lot about the economic problems in the West. I know that very few people in Denmark own a car. Only the wealthy can afford one."

"Excuse me!" I said with a laugh, "I'm not a rich man by any means, but I have *two!*"

He looked at me in disbelief. "But the workers don't have cars!"

"Of course they do. Many of them have two, and a house trailer or a boat—or both—to haul behind."

For the first time I saw a shadow of suspicion creep across his usually open face. Then he brightened again. "You're making a joke, of course."

"Fyodr, I'm only telling you the facts. That's the way it is in Western Europe. Of course in the United States a family may have three cars and a swimming pool, too."

He shook his head, unable to believe me. I had to convince him of my sincerity, or our discussion would be of no value. I broke the silence. "You don't always get the truth in your books and newspapers."

"Of course we do."

"I know you don't. You don't know what's going on outside your country, only what the state wants you to know. Everything you read, or hear, is censored."

"But the censors don't keep truth from us. They see that we get it. We need censors to protect us from capitalist propaganda and the stupid ideas of reactionaries."

"We have no censors in Denmark. Why should you need them here? What are the Soviets afraid of—besides the truth?"

Fyodr leaned forward and lowered his voice. "You think Russia is a Communist country...but it's not. We've only achieved socialism. Most of the people don't believe in communism even now. They have to be educated, and to do that the state must control what everyone reads."

"But is the state always right? Who decides? You allow no dissent, no exchange of opinions. Men like Solzhenitsyn, they can't get their writings published in your country."

"They're counter-revolutionaries—traitors. No individual has the right to think independently. We must work together. The censors see that we have unity. But when we've become a Communist country, then we won't need censors anymore because everyone will believe."

"So! Communism is a religion after all—something you 'believe.' "

He frowned and thought that one through. "Of course it's not a religion. That's absurd. I'm trying to think of how to say it in English. I'd call it a *faith*. I believe in communism, and history will prove we're right. We're in the stream of destiny. It's inevitable."

"I know that Marx and Engels believed that the onward march of socialism was inevitable, as though it were predestined. So did Lenin—except he wanted to help the trend along. But how can there be an inevitable destiny for human society? And why should there be?"

Fyodr shrugged. "It's just there, like evolution in animals. Man is a higher species, a social animal now, but still evolving."

"But in a predetermined direction? Toward a particular destiny? Is there some 'spirit' in history like the animists think lives in trees and rocks and sun? Could this destiny exist by chance? How—and why? I've never understood the thinking of a Communist on this point."

"I don't know, either," he replied thoughtfully. "That question has bothered me. I'm an atheist, a materialist—but I believe in a destiny for the human race, without any 'spirit' or god directing it." Again he shrugged expressively. "Like so many things, maybe there is no answer. For instance, the universe. It's just there. No one can explain it."

Fyodr was honest, willing to admit his doubts, and I

respected him for that. I wanted to say, "There is no explanation without God." But it was too early in our conversation. I would wait.

"You capitalists are dying out," he continued, when I said nothing. "Look around the world and see. Progressive socialism is taking over everywhere, and you can't stop it! There's the proof!"

"But you have your problems, too," I countered. "Everything isn't so rosy with the socialists. Marx and Lenin quarreled—as Russia and China do today. And you have a big problem with alcohol in your country. No drugs and prostitution, but lots of alcoholism."

"It's true," he admitted frankly, "but we haven't yet reached our goal. When we do, alcoholism will disappear. Alcohol won't be necessary. Like religion. Some people need it now to face their problems, but they won't when the world is one Communist state."

"I'll be honest, Fyodr. We visitors find many things we don't like about Russia."

"What?"

"The Iron Curtain. The restrictions here are like no other place in the world. The tight control on everything including people's thoughts—it's like entering a prison. You've destroyed private initiative and competition. Sales people in stores are rude. They couldn't care less whether you bought anything or not. Walk into a store in the West and you're waited on politely and helped because they want to sell you something. But *here*. . . !" I threw up my hands. "I feel like I'm offending them sometimes when I ask to see what they have for sale."

He laughed. "Oh, I get angry too. But that's the difference between our systems. Capitalism tries to sell people things they don't even need. But why should we do that? If you need something, then buy it. Every store is the same. They're all owned by the state as they should be and all get their merchandise from the same state-owned factories, so there's no competition, no reason for the workers in one store to try to get you to buy from them."

"Exactly—so they don't care. And it shows. They could at least be polite and human. Such stony faces!"

"But you capitalists pretend to be polite just to sell your products. You don't really care about people—just money!"

"Maybe there's some truth on both sides," I conceded and lapsed into silence again, thinking how difficult it was to discuss a thing when neither person could understand the other's point of view. Fyodr, however, was obviously enjoying the conversation immensely.

"Look what we've done with this country since the revolution!" he said, with visible pride. "Under the Czars the people had nothing!"

"They don't have much yet," I said bluntly. "Not compared with capitalist countries."

"Give us time. Soon there will be no capitalism, and then there will be no more taxes. That would be good news even for you...yes?"

"You think you pay no income tax in Russia?"

"I *know* it!"

"But I know you do! Everyone works for the state, and the taxes are taken out of your wages before you get them. Wages are *very* low here compared with other industrialized countries. And the state charges you a big profit on everything it sells you. The prices in your stores are outrageous, and the quality is poor. That's how you pay your taxes—big ones!"

He didn't look happy. "That's the way you see it, but still I don't pay any tax."

"Okay. Believe what you want to believe. Changing the subject a little, I've always wondered about those pictures of people I've seen in front of factories. Who are they?"

"Those are the best workers. It's a great honor. I'd love to have my picture in front of a factory someday!"

"Much cheaper than an increase in salary," I thought.

Aloud I said, "Is that the reward for working harder than anyone else?"

"Not a reward...." He frowned and thought for a moment. "I don't know how to express it in English too well, but it's an honor. We don't bribe workers here like you do in the West, where the wealthy exploit the masses and quiet their unrest with an occasional raise in salary while they pocket billions in profits for themselves. A good Communist works in order to serve the state—the common good—not to get a higher salary for himself. I believe in communism, and I want to give my life to advance social justice in the world."

"Fyodr, you're an idealist, and I respect you for that. But how many people feel that way?"

"It's true that many still have bourgeois ideas. But that will change with education. They don't know any better yet. That's why we still have restrictions, what you capitalists call an 'Iron Curtain.' We're building a society based on an ideology, and we must protect our people from false ideas. But one day these 'curtains' and borders won't be necessary."

"When will that be?"

"In fifty years we conquered half the world. Give us another fifty and we'll conquer the other half—maybe before—and then the world will be a paradise!"

I couldn't help smiling at his choice of words. "*Paradise*—how is it that an atheist uses a religious term?"

Fyodr gave a quick laugh. "Call it whatever you want. You know what I mean."

"But it's interesting to me," I said pointedly, "that when you want to describe the perfect society you're aiming for, you have to use a religious word—one that means 'heaven.' "

He laughed again and shrugged. "Words have a history, and this one comes from religion—but it's a word we understand."

I leaned forward in my chair to face him directly.

"Fyodr," I began in a very serious tone, "let me tell you something. You'll never conquer the world!"

"Of course we will! History is on our side!"

"No, you will not conquer, and I can tell you why."

"Why?"

"Because no one is good enough to live up to the high ideals of communism, to always share everything equally with others and work for the good of society instead of for selfish reasons."

His face had lost its confident expression, and he became very thoughtful. "You're right," he said at last with a heavy sigh. "We're not good enough. *I'm* not good enough. I try, but I can't succeed."

In that moment I felt a great love for Fyodr. He was an idealist, willing to work for the good of the state without getting anything for himself. But he was also honest—honest enough to admit that he hadn't been able to live up to his aspirations.

He was nodding his head, a solemn expression on his face. "I have thought of that, and you're right. That's the problem—we're not good enough. If we were good enough, we would have conquered already!"

"I know the solution, Fyodr."

"You do? What is it?" There was almost a childish eagerness in his voice.

"God sent His Son Jesus Christ to die for our sins, and when we receive Him into our hearts He makes new persons out of us."

Fyodr sat up with a jerk and looked at me in open-mouthed astonishment. "You're a Christian!" he half-whispered. "I never thought Christians were clever!"

"Thank you," I said with an embarrassed laugh, "but you don't have to be very clever to know that something's wrong inside that you have no power to make right. All men know this about themselves."

He was still looking at me in disbelieving shock. "Educated people like you are Christians in Denmark?"

he asked at last. "But in Russia no one believes in God. Our scientists. . ."

"That's not true," I interrupted. "Your own Ministry of Religion admits that over 60 percent of the people in Russia believe in God today."

"No, that's not possible!"

"I'm only telling you what the Ministry of Religion says."

"But where are they? Nearly all the churches are closed. Nobody goes except a few old women."

"That's not true, Fyodr. The government closed the churches, but the congregations still meet in secret. Last night I met for Bible study and prayer with Christian young people in a house not far from here.

Fyodr made no attempt to hide his astonishment. "*Young* people? You're telling me the truth? Why don't I ever meet any?"

"Because they're not allowed to talk about God to someone like you. They've been driven underground, persecuted, put in prison. But they still believe."

"They're not persecuted," he said indignantly. "We have freedom of religion. It's guaranteed in our constitution. If they would obey the laws they'd have no problem."

"Do you know the laws, and especially the regulations? What you call 'freedom of religion' allows them to be Christians in a church for a few hours each week but forbids them to be Christians anywhere else the rest of the week. They can't talk about God at home, at the factory, in a park, can't even carry a Bible on the street."

"Of course. That would be religious propaganda. We can't allow that in an atheist state!"

"Is that fair? Is it even human?"

"Why not!"

"You never saw the argument of Aida Skripnikova, a young Christian girl right here in your own city. Your papers wouldn't publish it, but she asked this question:

Would you be content to discuss theater only in a theater or sports only in a stadium? Then why must a Christian only be allowed to speak of God in a church? You can gather with your friends at any time to speak on any subject, but a Christian breaks the law if he visits a friend and they talk together of Jesus Christ who is life itself to them.' Is this just?''

Fyodr looked thoughtful. A struggle seemed to be going on inside, and I was sure that his sense of honesty and justice saw the truth in Aida's appeal.

"But socialism and communism are based upon *atheism*," he said at last. "We can't allow our goals to be destroyed by myths."

"What myths?"

"Well, believing in God and miracles."

"You believe in miracles—greater ones than any Christian believes in," I said quietly. "All atheists do."

"What do you mean?"

"Well, you believe that everything, this whole universe, came from nothing. Right? That's a bigger miracle than anything the Bible talks about."

He smiled weakly but said nothing. I continued. "You believe that life and intelligence sprang unassisted and by pure chance from dead, empty space. That's a much bigger miracle than anything I believe in!"

Fyodr laughed good-naturedly. "Maybe," he said thoughtfully. "Maybe you have a point."

"Well, that's what an atheist believes, isn't it?"

"We certainly don't believe in a 'creator.' "

"Do you have any scientific evidence that everything came from nothing and by pure chance without any intelligent direction? I don't ask if it makes sense, because it obviously doesn't. But has anything ever been observed in the laboratory that would bear this out, or isn't this contrary to all the natural laws we have discovered?"

He smiled sheepishly but made no reply.

"Fantastic miracles you atheists believe in! So don't look

down on Christians for believing in miracles. And how do you account for *your* miracles? The big explanation is—*chance!* Given enough time, 'nothing' turns into 'everything' by *chance!* Well, the miracles I believe in were done by a God of infinite wisdom and love. There *is* a destiny for humanity, because God has a plan for all who are willing to trust and obey Him. That's easier to believe and a much better explanation than what you believe!"

"I can't argue with your logic," Fyodr admitted frankly. "I never thought of it that way, but I guess atheism does accept some rather huge miracles, if by that you mean events beyond scientific explanation. I always accepted that science had done away with God by explaining everything without Him."

"Well, you know that's not true. Modern science is no closer to understanding the truth about this universe than the alchemists were. We've learned a lot, but what we don't know expands faster than our knowledge. Einstein said that the more science discovers, the more we are forced to believe in God."

"But religion is so impractical. The Bible says man doesn't need bread to live. Communism says bread is the main thing."

"That's another piece of false information you've been given," I replied earnestly. "The Bible, in fact, says that man needs bread. But Jesus said that man can't live by bread *alone*, because man is more than a lump of protein molecules with nerves. Man is also a spiritual being, and the evidence for that is your appreciation of beauty, justice, truth, love, purpose, none of which can be explained as mere chemical reactions in cells nor could they have been derived from some survival-of-the-fittest-natural-selection process. That part of man exists because God made us in His image. That's why God could become a man—and that's who Jesus was: God stepping into human history to reveal Himself to us."

Fyodr sat quietly for a few minutes, deep in thought.

At last he said, "The main thing is, I know I'm not good enough to live up to the high ideals of communism, and I'm interested in finding a solution. You say that Jesus was God becoming a Man to solve this problem for us. But how do I know Jesus really existed?"

I began to explain the historical evidence for Christ, and the evidence for His resurrection. I told him how Christ had changed my own life and that this was the only way to really change society—by making new men. I explained that communism could put a new suit of clothes on men, but that Jesus puts a new man inside the suit when a heart opens to Him.

Fyodr told me again that he had realized for a long time that the real problem lay within, but that at first he had thought this could be solved by determining to live the Communist ideology. But in moments of honesty he had been forced to admit it didn't work, either for him or for others. But he had buried these doubts in a fresh effort to try harder. We talked on past midnight, and Fyodr asked me to pray for him. After we had prayed together, he accepted a New Testament and said he would read it. That was a big step!

He didn't make a "decision" right then in the way we might expect in the West, but I am confident that Fyodr felt his need of Christ and took a first step toward becoming one of His followers that night. God's Word no doubt did the rest.

Someday I hope to meet Fyodr in "paradise."

18

Revolution of Love

"Hans, you've got to be kidding!" said Rene, looking at me skeptically. "You expect us to believe that a Russian delegation went to Sweden to learn how to destroy the church?"

Five of us, Rene and I, Johny Noer, Leon Have, and Johannes Facius were discussing what we could do to combat the deteriorating morals in Denmark.

"That's right," I replied. "The Soviet Ministry of Religion was so impressed with the decline of Christianity in Sweden that a team of its antireligious experts went there to learn the secret of secularization, Swedish style."

"That's really something!" exclaimed Johny. "What did they discover?"

"That I don't know, but I imagine they concluded that Sweden's route—its high standard of living, pleasure orientation, free sex, and pornography—are not what they want to use in Russia. They'll probably stick to their own methods."

These comments evoked a discussion that lasted for some time and always returned to the amazing fact that the church in Western Europe, with all its freedom to worship and evangelize anywhere and at any time, nevertheless seemed weaker than the persecuted church behind the Iron Curtain.

"In Russia the Communists preach materialism," I said, "but here the Christians live it. In the West we preach Christ, but there the believers live Christ."

"Do you want to know what really bothers me?" asked Rene. "The Communists have no basis for morals, because they don't believe in God. But they have enough sense to reject the degeneracy that is sweeping the West. You don't find drugs and prostitution and pornography and the worship of sex in those atheistic countries. But here in supposedly Christian Denmark, where 90 percent of the people belong to the church, we have become so decadent that we allow any kind of immorality and perversion—and even give it legal protection!"

That sparked a further heated discussion. Hadn't the Bible predicted this upsurge in wickedness as one of the signs preceding Christ's return? Then what responsibility did Christians have to actively oppose the amoral permissiveness which had become the accepted way of life for our generation? Shouldn't we just "preach Christ"? These questions were discussed in detail, particularly with reference to the new law that had recently legalized pornography in Denmark.

Eventually we concluded that something more than praying and talking had to be done, that as Christians we had the responsibility to take action. But how, and what?

"John the Baptist told Herod to his face that he was sinning against God when he took his brother's wife," I said. "That's what our generation needs to realize—that pornography, free sex, drugs, homosexuality, aren't just a matter of offending a few 'narrow-minded prudes.' They're an abomination to God, like Sodom and Gomorrah. We ought to have the guts to stand up for God's righteousness, but who would listen to us?"

"We've got to catch people's attention!" exclaimed Rene.

"That's right," added Johny, "and not be afraid of the consequences. Herod threw John in a dungeon and eventually cut off his head. The Christians in Communist countries are being imprisoned and even killed for their faith. I think it's to our shame that no one has put *us* in prison for our Christian testimony!"

Rene and I exchanged glances. This was something we had often discussed, and we had finally concluded that Christians in Denmark were not persecuted because Satan lets sleeping dogs lie. Apparently we weren't bothering our enemy, so he didn't bother us.

Johny was getting excited. "The way pornography warps and pollutes and turns the beauty God intended for sex and love into something ugly and degrading. . . we've got to do something about all those porno shops!"

"That's fine talk," said Johannes, who was less impulsive than the rest of us, "but what can we really do?"

"Why don't we paper up their windows some night?" I suggested. "Then no one could see into them."

"What would that accomplish?" commented Leon dryly. "They take the paper off and we've gone to a lot of trouble for nothing. It shouldn't be just plain paper."

"Slogans!" exclaimed someone. "Print Bible verses on the paper!" said someone else. There was enthusiastic laughter as we warmed to the idea. "Imagine a porno shop covered up with Bible verses!" We were all getting excited now and talking all at once.

"We've got to sign some name. Why? Well, people will want to know who did it. We shouldn't take credit for anything. Yes, but everyone should know it was done by Christians! How about signing the posters, 'Young Christians'!"

And so "The Young Christians" came into being.

Driven by a determination to let Denmark know that our deteriorating morals were an offense to the God who had created us, we contacted concerned young Christians in every city and town across our small country and

mobilized them secretly into an "army." One unforgettable morning at 3:00 A.M., across the length and breadth
of Denmark, the army attacked—with paste and posters,
and prayer.

Following their assignments with military precision,
teams of young people converged on pornography shops
wherever they were found, pasting their windows shut
with a poster we had mass-produced for the occasion. It
read, "Love is Pure," and was signed, "The Young
Christians." In Copenhagen alone about fifty shops were
plastered shut as well as scores in many other towns.
Some of the teams were arrested on the spot, and forced
to take the posters down. But other young people suddenly appeared on the deserted streets to paste the
windows shut again. At 5:00 A.M. calls were made to all
the newspapers telling what had been done.

Denmark awakened from its smug sleep later that
morning to find the startling news in many papers:
"Young Christians" had attacked pornography all over
the country. Of course the porno shops continued ped-
dling their filth. But we had exposed the issue and started
many people thinking about the degeneracy of our society.
Other demonstrations followed, and it was an exciting
new way, at least for Christians in Denmark, to let their
voices be heard in an attempt to arouse the public conscience. I managed to squeeze in time from my work to
take an active part with The Young Christians. After all,
our mission was interested in all of Europe, not just the
Communist countries.

Sonya and the other refugees were now living in
Sweden, working for a mission involved behind the Iron
Curtain. News of their remarkable escape had begun to
spread. As I traveled on speaking tours trying to raise
prayer and financial support for our persecuted brethren,
I would sometimes be approached after the service by

people begging me to bring their relatives out from behind closed borders, too.

"But I can't bring anyone across those borders!" I always replied.

"You did it once—and you could do it again!" I would be told.

"If you knew the whole story," I replied over and over, "you'd know that I only bungled it. God is the one who brought us all out safely. That was a unique situation. I don't expect Him ever to ask me to do it again, and I couldn't unless He told me to." I was more and more conscious of my part in a spiritual battle between God and Satan for the hearts and destiny of men and that I must take my orders from God.

At times I marvelled at the power and genius of Satan in his role as inspirer of an iron-fisted atheism's attempts to destroy Christianity through oppression in one part of the world, while promoting "freedom of expression" elsewhere in order to peddle his no-less-destructive licentious and poisonous pleasures. But I marvelled even more at the way God was able to use these very tactics of the enemy to expose the hypocrisy of a fat, decadent, and false Christianity, shaking everything that had no real foundation, while strengthening the true faith. I was beginning to see God's hand behind the scenes where I had never expected, nudging history along to its prophesied climax.

I began to feel a new responsibility to tell men and rulers everywhere that this earth belonged to the God who created it, and that one day, soon, His Son, King Jesus, was coming back. Not meekly, to submit to rejection and crucifixion again, but this time to reign in righteousness and power. We'd better prepare to meet our God!

Rene and I discussed a number of times the amazing similarity between what Satan was accomplishing in the East and in the West. The tactics were exactly opposite: oppression in one place and freedom to do anything in

the other. The end result, however, was the same. In
Russia, Christianity was limited to the church building
a few hours each week by laws and regulations forbidding
it to be practiced elsewhere. In Denmark, the practice of
Christianity was also largely confined to the church for
an equally small fraction of the week, but by our own
choice. We could cluck and feel piously sympathetic
toward those oppressed Christians who had so little
freedom and then voluntarily limit our Christianity in
practice to the unreasonable demands of their laws.
Denmark was in the "free world"—so our press and
political speeches boasted, unaware that we were the
slaves of sensuality.

I had long believed in living for Christ, but the conviction deepened within me that this must involve more than
a quiet display of Christian virtues. Christ had publicly
denounced the Pharisees and other religious hypocrites;
He had gone into the temple and driven out those who
had turned a house of prayer to their own profit. He had
ridden to the temple that day at the head of what our
generation would call a *demonstration*, as thousands lined
the streets shouting, "Glory to God," hailing Him as the
Son of David, the rightful King, and had followed Him
into Jerusalem, expecting Him to take the reins of
government.

He had refused to rebuke the crowd. In fact, He had
said that if they didn't speak, the stones themselves would
awake to cry out. To what extent the demonstration that
day had precipitated His crucifixion I did not know, but
He had given it His blessing. Many of us in Denmark felt
that it would be a shame for the cobblestones in our streets
to shout glory to God when there were Christians whose
voices should be heard. We began to lay plans for a public
demonstration that would say to Denmark: Repent—or
be judged!

The demonstration we visualized was going to be much
more than a simple march. It would continue from early

morning until late at night. We called it the "Long Day."
Johny Noer wanted it to include a "Jesus Festival" in one
of Copenhagen's best-known parks. I contacted Brother
Andrew, who was already widely respected in Denmark,
and he agreed to participate. Loren Cunningham offered
the help of Youth With A Mission.

The "Long Day" actually began the night before with
a service in the main Copenhagen cathedral. It seated
about 2,300, but 3,500 crowded into it that evening as
Brother Andrew called for Christians around the globe
to unite in a "Revolution of Love" that would tear this.
world out of the clutches of Satan and turn it over to Jesus
Christ. In Him alone a race alienated from its Creator
could be reconciled to God and thus to one another.

The next morning, August 11, 1972, nearly 1,000
gathered in a state church that seats about 650 and has
only a fraction of that number in attendance on a typical
Sunday morning. Many participated as we spent an hour
together asking God to grant our nation a revival of true
Christianity and to liberate our brethren in the East from
the chains of prison and persecution. About 100 teams
organized by Youth With A Mission were on the streets
of Copenhagen all day distributing 70,000 leaflets. In the
afternoon the festival was held in Felldpark. It didn't draw
a large crowd in comparison with similar events elsewhere, but Denmark is a small country, and nearly 7,000
people gathered that afternoon to sing together of the love
of Christ and to publicly proclaim that this world belongs
to Him and not to men or Satan.

Early that evening, following the festival, the Christians
began to gather again. A month before, we had told the
authorities there would be about 2,000 of us. That was
a large expectation for Copenhagen. The police divided
by four and decided they didn't need to bother with 500
peaceful marchers. As the crowd continued to swell, I ran
to a phone and called the officer on duty to say that there

were at least 5,000 of us and we would need some help with the traffic.

Red-faced and surprised, the motorcycle escort arrived and we began our march, winding through Copenhagen's historic streets for about two and a half miles. Along the route many others joined us, and when we reached the town-hall square, the crowd had grown to 10,000. Brother Andrew, Loren Cunningham, and Johny Noer spoke briefly about what it means to be a true Christian— allowing Christ to live and love through us. Again we heard about the "Revolution of Love" that would de-throne evil and crown King Jesus Lord of all. It was a dramatic event, like nothing Copenhagen had ever seen, and I felt deeply moved as I looked out over that vast crowd singing praises to God. My heart ached for Chris-tians who had never known such liberty as this—and for my own countrymen who had such an abundance of lib-erty, yet neglected or abused it.

In the audience that night were many young people who were leaving the next day for Munich to tell the athletes and spectators gathering from all over the world for the Olympia Games of the love of our Lord. Unknown to us, those games, designed to bring the world together, would be cruelly interrupted by a savage display of hatred and murder. The young people came forward and knelt on the steps of the town hall. Other Christians laid their hands on them as everyone gathered around and prayed that God would take them and use them and that they would become an army to spread the flame of His love, not just at Munich, but around the world. And then it was over. All too soon the "Long Day" had ended.

Standing on the top of those steps watching the crowd slowly and reluctantly disperse, I thought of another and considerably different demonstration that had taken place six years before in Russia. From all over the Soviet Union about 500 representatives from 400 unregistered Baptist congregations had converged on Moscow's Old Square—

where they had been joined by another 100 from Moscow's Baptist Church—to do the unthinkable and unheard of for Russia: to present a petition in a mass demonstration at the entrace to the offices of the Central Committee of the Communist Party. Their request that ten leaders be allowed to meet with Leonid Brezhnev, the chairman of the Central Committee, was refused, but they left a document begging for an end to religious persecution and for the release of their brethren inprisoned for their faith all over Russia.

The only answer to that petition, quietly, legally, respectfully, and even hopefully presented, had been the brutal beating and arrest of all 500 participants as they sang together of their pledge to bring the Good News of God's love revealed in Christ to a world ravaged by sin. Two of the national leaders of the unregistered Baptist congregations, Georgi Vins and Gennadi Krutchkov, sought by Soviet police for years, bravely presented themselves two days later at the offices of the Central Committee to plead for the release of their comrades—and were arrested on false charges. Some of the things these men had said later at their infamous trial in Moscow came back to me now:

> I'm happy that for my faith in God I could come to know imprisonment...those brethren who are at this moment in prisons and camps are suffering, not for having broken Soviet law, but for having been faithful to God and His church.... I stand before you with a calm and clear conscience.... I want to offer thanks to God that I am a Christian.... I do not see you, Comrade Judge, Comrade Prosecutor, as my enemies; you're my brothers in the human race.... I shall pray to God for you in my cell.... Fresh persecution will only strengthen faith and witness God's eternal truth before generations yet

to come. . . . Today here, as in Pilate's day, Christ
our Saviour is being judged. . . .

I thought of Jews in the Soviet Union at that very
moment denied emigration to Israel and expelled from
their jobs for having requested it, then threatened with
imprisonment for having no gainful employment. I
thought of the 400 members of Georgi Vins' congregation, refused registration year after year and set upon and
beaten by the KGB as they met to worship in a woods
near Kiev the Sunday following his arrest. I thought, too,
of the writers Andrei Sinyavsky and Yuli Daniel, imprisoned in 1966, and the courage of other writers, scientists, and intellectuals such as Ginsburg, Galanskov,
Sakharov, Solzhenitsyn, and Medvedev, who had taken
up the battle for human rights at great risk to themselves.
Lists of names of tortured prisoners of conscience,
compiled by the courageous Council of Prisoners' Relatives and smuggled out to the West, hung like a weight
on my mind.

Memories poured over me—a handleless broom being
pushed along a gutter in Bulgaria by a saint in patches;
congregations denied a place to meet for worship, then
arrested for meeting illegally; of pastors driven, by threats
of imprisonment, to compromise Christ's commands, then
tortured by their consciences; the lies about "religious
freedom" spread by church leaders traveling in the West;
hands reaching out for Bibles; hundreds of thousands of
the victims of persecution crying out to God and to man
for help.

Ten thousand of us that evening in Copenhagen's town
hall square had sung of Christ and dedicated ourselves
to a "Revolution of Love" to carry His life and love to
the world. Would those words prove empty, or would we
make good our pledge in the power of the Holy Spirit?
The answer depended upon how much we really cared,
how deep our love.

I moved across the square in the wake of the thinning mass of Christians. Here was but a handful. There were millions of others around the world. If only we would rise up and *act*, in *love*! It could happen—and it *must*!

Epilogue

The years since I put on paper the incredible story of one Dane's mission to penetrate communism's "impossible" borders with the gospel of Jesus Christ have seen more miracles and triumphs (and some costly but instructive failures as well) than several additional books could contain. I have watched the growth of Dansk Europamission and followed with great interest the persistent, prayerful, and often daring innovations that have kept Bibles and other literature and financial aid flowing steadily behind the Iron Curtain in spite of Communist ingenuity and determination to stop it. Of course the full details of this secret invasion can never be published.

My wife, Ruth, and I had the opportunity in the summer of 1985 of once again visiting Hans and Ninna Kristian and spending some time at their mission headquarters in Denmark. We also had the privilege of going on a brief assignment as temporary mission "couriers." It was thrilling to experience again God's miraculous care in the process of making a "delivery" into the Soviet Union. Not that we eagerly jumped at the opportunity; in fact, we shrank from it. Yet we could not out of fear for our own personal safety turn a deaf ear to the cry of those who suffer so much and are in such deep need.

For propaganda purposes, well-known and well-meaning Western evangelists are periodically allowed to make "official" red-carpet visits and even to preach the gospel in Communist countries. The false impression of religious freedom given by the enthusiastic reports of such rare events is eagerly received by Westerners who seem unable to face the shocking truth. The truth can easily be discovered by anyone who attempts to penetrate the Iron Curtain with even one Bible. The crude and vicious treatment such a person receives contrasts with the benign smiles and deceitful handshakes extended to visiting religious dignitaries by Communist leaders whose sworn goal is to stamp out all religion.

Take for example the American couple that was detained for 21 hours for questioning at the Leningrad airport and then sent back to Finland because they each had one Russian Bible in their luggage. One week after that incident I had three Russian Bibles—two in my baggage and one in a hip pocket—when Ruth and I drove up to the Finnish-Soviet border north of Leningrad. We had discussed whether we ought to take any Bibles at all. Getting a different cargo through was our main assignment. The discovery of even one Bible could be disastrous. "Take as many as you have faith for," we had been told, "but don't jeopardize your main mission."

"This is for a pastor presently in prison, due to be released soon. And here's his wife's name and address—we'd like it delivered to her." That Bible was like nothing I had ever seen printed in Russian, a special study edition, oversized and in a zippered case. It obviously increased our risk, but it was a great privilege to take in something for which this dedicated and suffering leader had prayed for many years.

"How does a sun-tanned couple from Southern California traveling in *August* explain a dozen heavy winter coats in their luggage? And fur-lined ones, yet." Ruth and I had gone over that question a number of times to be certain that we would both give the same answer in case we were interrogated separately. What we must not disclose was the fact that the coats were for designated families of prisoners. I had memorized the recipients' strange names and addresses and maps for finding them before destroying all incriminating notes and documents.

"And what about that monster in the backseat?" That question was even more worrisome. It was hoped that somehow the border guards would think we were carrying an unusually large tape recorder and would not notice that it was actually a combination duplicator and shortwave radio as well—unavailable in the USSR and extremely useful to Christians for taping and duplicating broadcasts from the West.

Finding my wife's English Bible in her suitcase brought an angry and excited reaction from the guards, which anyone who has never experienced it would find incomprehensible and frightening. When my English Bible was discovered a few moments later, the atmosphere became extremely tense and the guards began to speak of us contemptuously among themselves as *religious.* Now they were like bloodhounds hot on a scent as they went through our remaining luggage. Every scrap of paper was removed from my briefcase, carefully examined, and tossed disdainfully in a heap. Then the empty briefcase was x-rayed for hidden compartments. The cassette tapes were found, taken to a back room, and within minutes the report came out that they contained hymns, Bible reading, and preaching in Russian. The hushed consultations and contemptuous treatment which followed that whispered report made us feel like criminals who had already been convicted.

Of course they found the two Russian Bibles in my luggage, which I insisted in my broken Russian were necessary for my study of that difficult language. I explained that the *study* Bible was especially helpful in *studying* Russian. The official in charge, a woman with steely eyes that seemed to look right through us, made it clear that she thought I was lying. By this time our rented car was being meticulously dismantled by two mechanics who were obviously specialists at finding hidden Bibles in vehicles.

Our mission looked like a total failure. Everything we had hoped to take across the border had been exposed to view—except for the third Bible in my hip pocket which, by God's grace, had been missed when I'd been patted down in a body search. "I'm the world's worst smuggler, Lord," I confessed, "but for the sake of those who need what we're carrying, please get it through."

I had no idea how such an impossible prayer could be answered. The experts had told us that if we were allowed to enter the USSR, the Bibles and anything else discovered would be noted on our passports and would have to be shown again when we exited the country. That would mean complete failure.

"Pack everything up!" The sudden announcement surprised me. I looked inquiringly at the interpreter, who was now wearing the official Intourist smile. "Yes, of course," she assured me, "you can go on to Leningrad now."

Back in the car and on our way at last with the border receding safely into the distance, I checked our passports and visas. Inexplicably, nothing had been written on them. We had passed the border with our precious cargo still intact! Overwhelmed with wonder and gratitude, we praised God for His grace and this fresh evidence that He cares for His own, and that the power of godless governments is helpless to frustrate His purpose.

The frightening and even impossible situations we faced in the process of completing the delivery and the many further evidences of God's miraculous care are all beyond the scope of a brief epilogue. Ruth and I felt less than heroic when it was all over. Hans Kristian and his mission had provided us the opportunity to be fellow workers in this one brief foray over Communist borders. He had been arrested eleven times in the course of his travels behind the Iron Curtain, while we had merely endured the normal tension and harassment. God had graciously allowed us to experience for ourselves once again the miracle of a successful Eastern European delivery. We were grateful for that and for another opportunity to learn more of the plight of suffering Christians in the USSR.

It was shocking to realize that somehow in the intervening years since our last visit to Eastern Europe we had almost forgotten our brothers and sisters over there. Now, once again, we had seen for ourselves and had ears to hear their heart cry: "Don't forget us! Please pray for us! And please bring us Bibles!"

In response to that cry—and in spite of Soviet ingenuity and determination to stop the flow—the amount of literature going in has been tremendous. The impressive statistics, however, don't begin to reveal the complexity of the task. In the Soviet Union, Russian is only one of the 131 different languages spoken and read. Most of the people have never had one single verse of the Scripture in their own tongue. To date the mission has reached 30 of these language groups with translations and is now working on 20 additional languages.

Labeled "pariahs," "leeches," and "social parasites"—with charitable donations for their support strictly forbidden—the plight of leaders in the unregistered church and that of their families is often pitiful. Dansk Europamission clandestinely sends in the needed funds to make subsistence possible for many of these hunted pastors and their wives and children. The families of martyrs and prisoners are being supplied as well with material relief.

A very important extension to the work occurred as an aftermath of Hans Kristian's second tour of the United States in 1974. On that occasion a young lawyer (at the time the city attorney of Denton, Texas) was so gripped by the urgency of Han's message that he, like the transformed fishermen of biblical times, "forsook all and followed Him." Today he heads the American affiliate of Dansk Europamission called Mission Possible which, since its inception, has placed more than 1,000,000 pieces of literature into the hands of Eastern European believers.

Since 1975 Hans Kristian has been a member of the International Sakharov Committee and is presently its vice president. It is a very vocal human rights organization and exposes through parliamentary hearings and press conferences around the world the blatant violations of human rights prevalent in Communist countries. The speedy and effective dissemination of information was further enhanced in 1981 when a press bureau was set up in Copenhagen, whereby Hans could inform the world media by telex of current developments in the Communist world.

Hans was one of the first Christians to enter newly opened China and to bring back to the church in the West accurate news of conditions there. Today Dansk Europamission makes more than five hundred trips per year into China, bringing Bibles and Christian literature. The mission is also instrumental in providing religious broadcasting to millions of Chinese listeners.

The nerve center of the work today is an old three-story white stucco house on a quiet residential street of a Copenhagen suburb. Hans Kristian's family home is a few steps away across the Danish-green lawn in back, which is dotted with apple trees and surrounded with neatly trimmed hedges.

Stepping inside the unimposing offices, one senses a quiet intensity in the atmosphere. Minutes count. Lives and souls are at stake. A warfare is being waged on a level which requires the utmost sensitivity and spiritual discernment. It is both a house of prayer and a place of movement and energy. Han's pre-dawn arrival gives him much-needed time for preparation in prayer and the reading of God's Word. Ninna has left the house even earlier to clean the rooms at a local school. Then she, too, is there to lend a hand when the mission offices open. Somehow she finds time as well to keep an immaculate home for Hans and their four children and to prepare gourmet candlelight dinners for hungry visitors.

For most Christians in the West the realities that their spiritual brothers and sisters in Communist bloc countries experience are scarcely comprehensible. To exist year after year in the worst kind of spiritual poverty, to be perhaps the only believer in an isolated Siberian village, to see your children pressured day and night to embrace a godless ideology, to live without the comfort and instruction of a single printed page of Scripture—the gulf between our comprehension and their experience is too vast to fathom.

There are men and women and young people today who have counted the cost of identifying with Christ and His people and who desire with all their hearts to live, and if need be to die, by His holy Word. Shouldn't we be willing to be fellow laborers with those who, at great cost, are placing His Word into outstretched hands?

A mistake that we often make in the West—and sometimes as the result of reading a book like this—is to look upon suffering Christians in Communist countries as super-saints who see so many miracles that they are immune to ordinary temptations. On the contrary, God cares for them because of their great need and simple faith, not because they have reached some higher level of spirituality. Their vulnerability is tragically apparent, not only in the many Maria Brauns we never hear of, but in the families of those Christians who either escape or are granted visas to the West. Young people who have resisted the frontal assault of persecution under Communist governments often succumb to the subtle temptations of Western prosperity and its accompanying vices such as drugs, pornography, and free sex. Increasing numbers of these immigrant families who carefully protected their children in Communist lands only to lose them in the West need our earnest prayers and help.

If you would like further information about the work recounted in this book and opportunities for your personal involvement (such as names and addresses of Christians in prison to correspond with), write to:

Mission Possible
Box 2014
Denton, Texas 76201